Sunset

GARDEN WATERING SYSTEMS

BY SUSAN LANG AND THE EDITORS OF SUNSET BOOKS

SUNSET BOOKS · MENLO PARK, CALIFORNIA

MAKING SENSE OF WATERING

When you supply your plants with suitable amounts of water at timely intervals, they will show their appreciation in the form of healthy growth, impressive blooms, and delectable fruit. A well-planned, well-maintained watering system will help you deliver the required water efficiently, with a minimum of waste. It will also make your life a little easier, leaving you more time to plant, putter, and generally enjoy your garden.

This book provides detailed information on watering systems, from basic components including portable sprinklers and soaker hoses to sophisticated underground sprinkler and drip setups. It also provides the knowledge you need to operate a system effectively—from tips on using water wisely to a discussion of your soil's important role in irrigation, and from the "how much" and "how often" of watering to the best ways to water common types of plantings.

We gratefully acknowledge Tom Bressan of The Urban Farmer and David Zoldoske of the Center for Irrigation Technology for their guidance and review of the manuscript. Additionally, thanks go to Tom Ash of the Irvine Ranch Water District and Gary Banuelos of the USDA for their helpful advice.

SUNSET BOOKS

Vice President, Sales: Richard A. Smeby
Vice President, Editorial Director: Bob Doyle
Production Director: Lory Day
Art Director: Vasken Guiragossian

Staff for this book:

Managing Editor: Susan Bryant Caron
Sunset Books Senior Editor, Gardening: Suzanne Normand Eyre
Copy Editor and Indexer: Pamela A. Evans
Photo Researcher: Tishana Peebles
Production Coordinator: Patricia S. Williams
Special Contributors: Lisa Anderson, Jean Warboy
Proofreader: Jan deProsse, Eagle Eye Editorial Services

Art Director: Alice Rogers
Illustrator: Rik Olsen
Additional Illustrators: Jane McCreary, Mimi Osborne, Mark Pechenik, Reineck & Reineck
Computer Production: Fog Press, Linda Bouchard

Cover: Side view of an underground lawn sprinkler system. Photography by Norman A. Plate. Border photograph of wild ginger *(Asarum canadense)* by David Cavagnaro.

PHOTOGRAPHERS

William D. Adams: 15, 72 bottom right, 100, 107; **Em Ahart:** 19, 31, 36 left and bottom right, 37, 40 bottom, 47 top right, 54, 56 top and bottom left, 58 bottom right (all), 67 top, 70 top and middle left, 72 top right, 79 left, 80 top left (all), 82 bottom left, top and bottom right, 83 top, 86 left, 102 top; **William H. Allen, Jr.:** 49 right, 63; **Curtis Anderson:** 57 top right, 58 middle and bottom left; **Aquapore Moisture Systems, Inc.:** 48 bottom left, 51 top right, 72 bottom left; **Marion Brenner:** 12 bottom left and center; **David Cavagnaro:** 24, 30 bottom; ©**Van Chaplin/Southern Living, Inc.:** 3 bottom right, 96; **Peter Christiansen:** 48 right; **Crandall & Crandall:** 7 right, 17 top, 18 top right, 29 bottom left, 39 bottom left, 41, 58 top right; **Claire Curran:** 12 middle left; ©**Alan and Linda Detrick:** 7 left, 50 bottom right, 93 top right; **Gardener's Supply Co.:** 49 left; **David Goldberg:** 21 bottom right (both), 25 bottom; **Philip Harvey:** 29 bottom right; **Saxon Holt:** 13, 18 bottom left, 74, 93 bottom right; **Hunter Industries:** 36 top right, 52 top, 55 right, 66 right, 87; **Ben Klaffke:** 34, 59, back cover top left; **Robert Kourik/TerraInforma Communications:** 3 middle right, 39 right, 44, 52 bottom, 72 top and middle left, 73 left, 77, 78 top; **Janet Loughrey:** 3 bottom left, 6 top left, 88; **Ray Maleike:** 25 top; **Charles Mann:** 12 top left and right, 106 top; **Chas. McGrath:** 103; **L. R. Nelson Corporation:** 57 left, 65 left, 86 right, 99 left; **Olson Irrigation Systems:** 67 bottom, 83 bottom; **Gary Parker:** 57 bottom right; **Jerry Pavia:** 18 top left; **Norman A. Plate:** 1, 10, 47 top left and bottom right, 56 bottom right (both), 68 right, 70 bottom right, 72 middle right, 80 bottom right, 81, 84, 85 left, 93 top left, 99 right, 101, 104 left, 108 left, 109 left; **Rich Pomerantz:** 73 top right; **Rob Proctor:** 21 top left; **Rain Bird:** 55 left, 58 top left, 91, 110; **Ian Reeves:** 46 bottom, 69 right, 71 bottom left and right, 78 bottom, 93 bottom left, 94; **Bill Ross—Westlight Photography:** 6 top right, 106 bottom; **Phillip C. Roullard:** 47 bottom left (all), 70 bottom left, 71 top right; **Richard Shiell:** 28, 66 top and bottom left; **Southern Living, Inc.:** 90; **Lauren Springer:** 3 top right, 22; **Michael S. Thompson:** 3 top left, 4, 6 bottom, 9, 17 bottom, 29 top, 30 top, 35, 38 bottom, 46 top, 48 top left, 50 top left, 51 bottom right, 85 bottom right, 92, 102 bottom, 108 right; **Toro Company:** 38 top; **Deidra Walpole Photography:** 14; **Darrow M. Watt:** 51 left, 68 bottom left, 104 right, 105, 109 bottom right, back cover right; **Peter O. Whitely:** 3 middle left, 32; ©**Craig D. Wood:** 2, 16, 39 top left, 40 top, 48 middle left, 50 middle and top right, 56 top right (both), 64 left, 68 top left, 69 left, 70 top right, 71 top left (both) and middle left, 73 bottom right, 79 center and bottom right (both), 80 top right, 82 top left, 85 top right, 98, 109 top right, back cover bottom left; **Tom Wyatt:** 42, 50, bottom left, 62, 64 right (all), 65 top and bottom right, 79 top right, 95.

Contents

Water is an essential part of gardening. Just as human beings need water to survive, so do plants—even the most drought-tolerant types. But how we water, and especially how much

USING WATER
WISELY

water we apply, has become an issue in many climates, not just in the most arid. Even gardeners in some regions with normally rainy summers have recently experienced watering restrictions during short droughts, as climatic patterns fluctuate around the globe.

If you've never had to pay dearly for your water or been restricted to watering only, say, on odd or even days, you still have good reason to practice water conservation. As you'll discover in this book, thoughtful irrigation offers more than just a hedge against water shortages.

A waterwise approach promotes a healthier garden, because it calls for giving plants just the amount of moisture they need and avoids both over- and underwatering. It can also free you to concentrate on the more enjoyable aspects of gardening. For example, if you're in the habit of dragging out garden hoses and watering all your plants by hand, perhaps you long for the freedom of a more efficient, automated watering system. Or, if mowing a spacious lawn strikes you as drudgery, you may be happier with a smaller, easier-to-maintain lawn that consumes less water.

A watering can stands in for nature during dry weather.

These gardens in the Northwest (left) and the Southwest (right) are waterwise without sacrificing beauty or variety. Each one features plants adapted to the climate in which they are growing.

AN ATTITUDE CHANGE

Why have so many home gardeners—and not just in the arid West—become water conscious? Instead of allowing garden water to gush unregarded, they're using drip emitters that dispense water in drops, soaker hoses that slowly ooze moisture, and sprinklers governed by timers and rain override devices.

These changes have come about as people increasingly realize that water is a costly and limited resource that should be used sensibly. How far you go in making your garden waterwise usually depends on where you live.

Most western gardeners, for instance, work in a climate characterized by low rainfall, a long dry season, or both. Well over half of the West's home gardeners spend a good part of each year watering plants. The amount of garden water available to them is bound to decrease as the population grows and more people draw from a virtually fixed water supply.

During a dry year in Oregon's Cascade Range, drought lowered the water level of this reservoir to the original river bed.

Given that situation, it's not surprising that the West gave birth to *xeriscaping*, a term coined for water-efficient gardening (from the Greek word *xeros*, meaning dry). The idea was born in Colorado in 1981, following several years of drought in the Rocky Mountains, the High Plains, and California. The gist is to live within your region's means—that is, to favor native and other plants thriving on little or no irrigation beyond what nature normally supplies, and to knowledgeably ration the garden water you do apply. The waterwise concept has taken root throughout the West, as professional growers and home gardeners alike perceive that working in harmony with nature is both easier and thriftier than fighting it.

The notion has since spread to other regions that sometimes lack enough water to go around. They may experience short droughts, when normally abundant rainfall is skimpy, or peak water shortages in summer, when too many people place demands on the water system at one time. Water districts in these areas are assuming a leading role in promoting water-efficient gardening in their communities. Their efforts, along with occasional shortages that have resulted in watering restrictions or worse—watching gardens die—have convinced many residents of these areas to be more prudent in their use of water.

In their conservation programs, water districts usually target lawn irrigation first, because turf tends to cover the largest area in home landscapes. Most lawns not only require proportionately more water than other garden plantings, but are also typically overwatered. Studies conducted in the West show that as much as half the water consumed in a typical single-family residence ends up outdoors—mostly on lawns—and that homeowners apply at least twice the water their lawns really need. That pattern is not unique to the West—in Missouri, for example, outdoor watering accounts for as much as 80 percent of household water use in the summer, and most of that ends up on lawns.

A primary goal of waterwise gardening, no matter where it is practiced, is to give plants only the amount of moisture they require for healthy growth. Water is essential to plant life: it transports nutrients from the soil up into the plant; it is a key ingredient in photosynthesis, the process by which plants manufacture their own food; and it cools plants as it evaporates from their leaves. (See the chapter beginning on page 23 for more about plants' use of water.) But just because water is good for plants doesn't mean that more is better. In addition to being wasteful, excessive applications of water can harm or even kill plants—yet overwatering of every kind of planting is common in all regions.

Fortunately, just about any garden can be made more water efficient. Gardeners planning a new landscape can follow waterwise principles; see page 10. Homeowners with an established garden can gradually revamp it to make it more water conserving; see page 21. Water thriftiness is relative, though—how frugal you become usually depends on your climate and the amount of moisture you can expect from nature.

WHERE YOUR WATER GOES

You may not think you're using much water when you sprinkle the lawn or let the hose run into a collection of container plantings, but you're probably consuming it at a higher rate than you imagine. Here are some revealing statistics about typical garden water use.

❧ A 20- by 40-foot area of lawn needs 2,000 to 4,200 gallons of water a month, in the form of either rain or irrigation water. In a climate with rainy summers, nature will provide much of that moisture; in an arid or semiarid region, the homeowner has to provide most or all of it. In dry weather, gardeners in cool-summer areas can get by with less irrigation than can their counterparts in hotter climates.

The output rates of standard sprinklers are measured in gallons per minutes (gpm), whereas those of drip devices are measured in gallons per hour (gph).

❧ A standard full-circle lawn sprinkler emits 2 to 4 gallons every minute it's in operation.

❧ Drip emitters deliver water slowly—each one will dispense just ½ to 2 gallons of water per hour.

❧ A ½-inch-diameter garden hose (without a nozzle or sprinkler at the end) delivers up to about 300 gallons of water per hour; a ⅝-inch-diameter hose, to about 500 gallons per hour; and a ¾-inch-diameter hose, as much as 600 gallons per hour.

❧ A faucet with a slow-dripping leak can waste 350 gallons a month; one with a fast leak, about 600 gallons a month.

Water conservation isn't a concern limited to the arid and semiarid West. Here, water conservation principles are put into practice at a demonstration garden in Cape May, New Jersey.

Average Inches of Rain West and East of the 100th Meridian

WESTERN CITIES	MAY	JUNE	JULY	AUG.	SEPT.	OCT.	MAY–OCT.	FULL YEAR
Billings	2.39	2.07	.85	1.05	1.26	1.16	8.78	15.09
Boise	1.21	.95	.26	.40	.58	.75	4.15	11.71
Colorado Springs	2.28	2.02	2.85	2.61	1.31	.78	11.85	15.42
El Paso	.24	.56	1.60	1.21	1.42	.70	5.33	7.82
Los Angeles	.23	.03	.00	.12	.27	.21	.86	14.85
Phoenix	.14	.17	.74	1.02	.64	.63	2.71	7.11
Portland	2.08	1.47	.46	1.13	1.61	3.05	9.80	37.39
Reno	.74	.34	.30	.27	.30	.34	2.29	7.49
Salt Lake City	1.47	.97	.72	.92	.89	1.14	6.11	15.31
San Diego	.24	.06	.01	.11	.19	.33	.94	9.32
San Francisco	.35	.15	.04	.08	.24	1.09	1.95	19.33
Seattle	1.58	1.38	.74	1.27	2.02	3.43	10.42	38.60

EASTERN CITIES	MAY	JUNE	JULY	AUG.	SEPT.	OCT.	MAY–OCT.	FULL YEAR
Atlanta	4.02	3.91	4.73	3.41	3.17	2.53	21.27	48.61
Boston	3.52	2.92	2.68	3.68	3.41	3.36	19.57	43.81
Chicago	3.15	4.08	3.63	3.53	3.35	2.28	20.02	33.34
Cleveland	3.30	3.49	3.37	3.38	2.92	2.45	18.91	35.40
Dallas	4.27	2.59	2.00	1.76	3.31	2.47	16.40	29.45
Duluth	3.15	3.96	3.96	4.12	3.26	2.21	20.66	29.68
Miami	6.53	9.15	5.98	7.02	8.07	7.14	43.89	57.55
New Orleans	5.07	4.63	6.73	6.02	5.67	2.66	30.78	59.74
New York City	3.46	3.15	3.67	4.32	3.48	3.24	21.32	42.82
Norfolk	3.75	3.45	5.15	5.33	4.35	3.41	25.44	45.22
Omaha	4.33	4.08	3.62	4.10	3.50	2.09	21.72	30.34
St. Louis	3.54	3.73	3.63	2.55	2.70	2.32	18.47	33.91

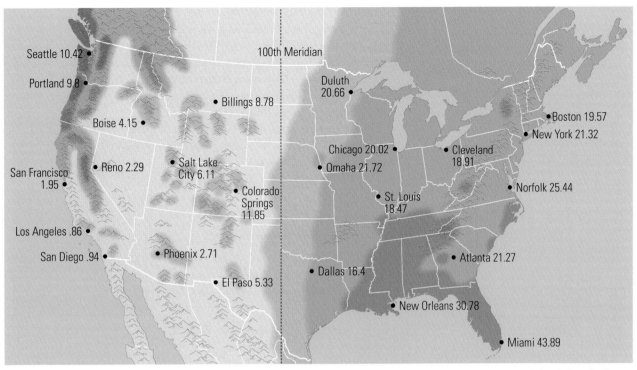

Seattle 10.42
Portland 9.8
100th Meridian
Duluth 20.66
Billings 8.78
Boise 4.15
Boston 19.57
New York 21.32
Chicago 20.02
Cleveland 18.91
San Francisco 1.95
Reno 2.29
Salt Lake City 6.11
Omaha 21.72
Norfolk 25.44
Colorado Springs 11.85
St. Louis 18.47
Los Angeles .86
San Diego .94
Phoenix 2.71
Atlanta 21.27
El Paso 5.33
Dallas 16.4
New Orleans 30.78
Miami 43.89

The map above shows the average number of inches of rainfall recorded by weather stations in 24 cities between May 1 and October 31. Of those cities, 12 are located east of the 100th meridian, the other 12 west of it.

The numbers clearly indicate how much drier the West is than the East during those critical 6 months. (The darkest shadings on the map correspond to the greatest annual rainfall.)

HELP FROM NATURE

How much irrigating you must do hinges largely on how much water is provided by nature and when it comes. Fog and snow melt provide some moisture, but nature's main contribution to gardens is rain—most importantly, the rain that falls during the warmer months of the year, when plants need it most.

The amount of yearly rainfall varies greatly from place to place. Generally, the eastern half of the continent has received enough—sometimes too much—rain. But regions within that half can sometimes go several years without getting enough water to supply their residents' needs.

The "generally-gets-enough-water" area extends from the Atlantic Ocean west across the Mississippi and Missouri Rivers to a north-south line very close to the 100th meridian (or 100° west longitude). That line runs through the middle of Texas (near Abilene), forms the eastern edge of the panhandle of Oklahoma, extends through western Kansas, and continues up through the middle of Nebraska, South Dakota, and North Dakota into Manitoba. As you approach the line, proceeding from east to west, rainfall gradually becomes chancier.

West of that line, rainfall drops off significantly. In most of the low elevations of Washington, Oregon, and California, the limited-water picture includes another characteristic: almost all of the precipitation—mainly in the form of rain—occurs between late fall of one year and late spring of the next. In other, generally higher elevations, precipitation is scattered to some degree around the calendar; even so, it doesn't add up to the more evenly distributed, more abundant precipitation east of the 100th meridian. In the deserts of the Southwest, what little rain falls often comes in relatively few heavy downpours.

In dry-summer regions of the West, automatic irrigation is practically indispensable for watering plants needing more moisture than is provided by nature. But it's also useful in some of the rainier areas with sandy soils that dry out quickly—stretches of the eastern seaboard, for example, including Cape Cod and Long Island. Even when rain falls in summer in these and other eastern regions, you can't always count on it falling on schedule to coincide with the needs of thirsty lawns and vegetable beds.

Rainfall seldom takes care of all of your plants' moisture needs.

PROTECTING PLANTS FROM DRYING WINDS

Strong winds can quickly rob plants of moisture, but you can protect them with a windbreak—a barrier that slows or dissipates wind.

A solid barrier like the fence above makes a poor windbreak. Because wind "flows" like water, it comes over the top of a solid barrier in a wave, crashing down on the other side.

The best type of windbreak is one that lets some wind pass through, such as the lattice fence above or the tall informal hedge below. As the wind filters through the fence openings or shrub branches, it loses force.

DEALING WITH DROUGHT

All regions experience occasional dry periods that may last weeks, months, or years. The word *drought* is most often used in reference to the West, but it is just as applicable to the eastern half of the continent (though dry spells there tend to be brief and in summer only). In areas of the West where summer dryness is the norm, droughts occur whenever winter precipitation is lower than usual and insufficient water accumulates in reservoirs.

You'll have an advantage during a prolonged dry spell if you've already instituted waterwise practices. Here are some additional measures to help you keep your garden going during a drought.

Mow higher during drought.

- Don't fertilize your plants. Fertilizer promotes new growth, which demands water.

- Mow your lawn less often and set the mower blades higher, though not more than twice the recommended mowing height (see page 20).

- Pull weeds; they compete with desirable plants for any available moisture.

- Irrigate carefully to avoid waste. Don't water between plants if you're watering by hand, and make sure any automated systems are operating efficiently.

- Apply water only to a plant's root zone—deeper irrigation wastes water. A soil probe is a good way to check on moisture at the root zone (see page 93).

- Try extending the time between waterings for as long as your plants look presentable.

- Keep a couple of buckets in the bathroom and let them fill with water as you're showering.

- Consider setting up a gray water system, which diverts runoff from the shower, bathtub, bathroom sink, and washing machine drains and delivers it to the garden; see page 42 for details.

- In a severe drought, stop watering your lawn; use available water to preserve any trees, shrubs, or other plants that you particularly favor. (However, think twice before watering a tree or shrub that has been in the ground for more than 2 years.)

WATERWISE PRINCIPLES

A waterwise approach to gardening doesn't mean growing plants that can survive bone-dry conditions—unless those are the circumstances under which you normally garden. Though to some, "waterwise garden" may conjure up images of a yardful of cacti or vast stretches of gravel, actually such a garden can be of any style. The key is to plant species that will thrive in your general climate as well as in your property's microclimates—all of the little climates-within-climates created by changes in elevation, prevailing winds, and sun and shade patterns.

HYDROZONING

The plan illustrated here was designed for a southwestern garden, but the concept can be applied to gardens anywhere.

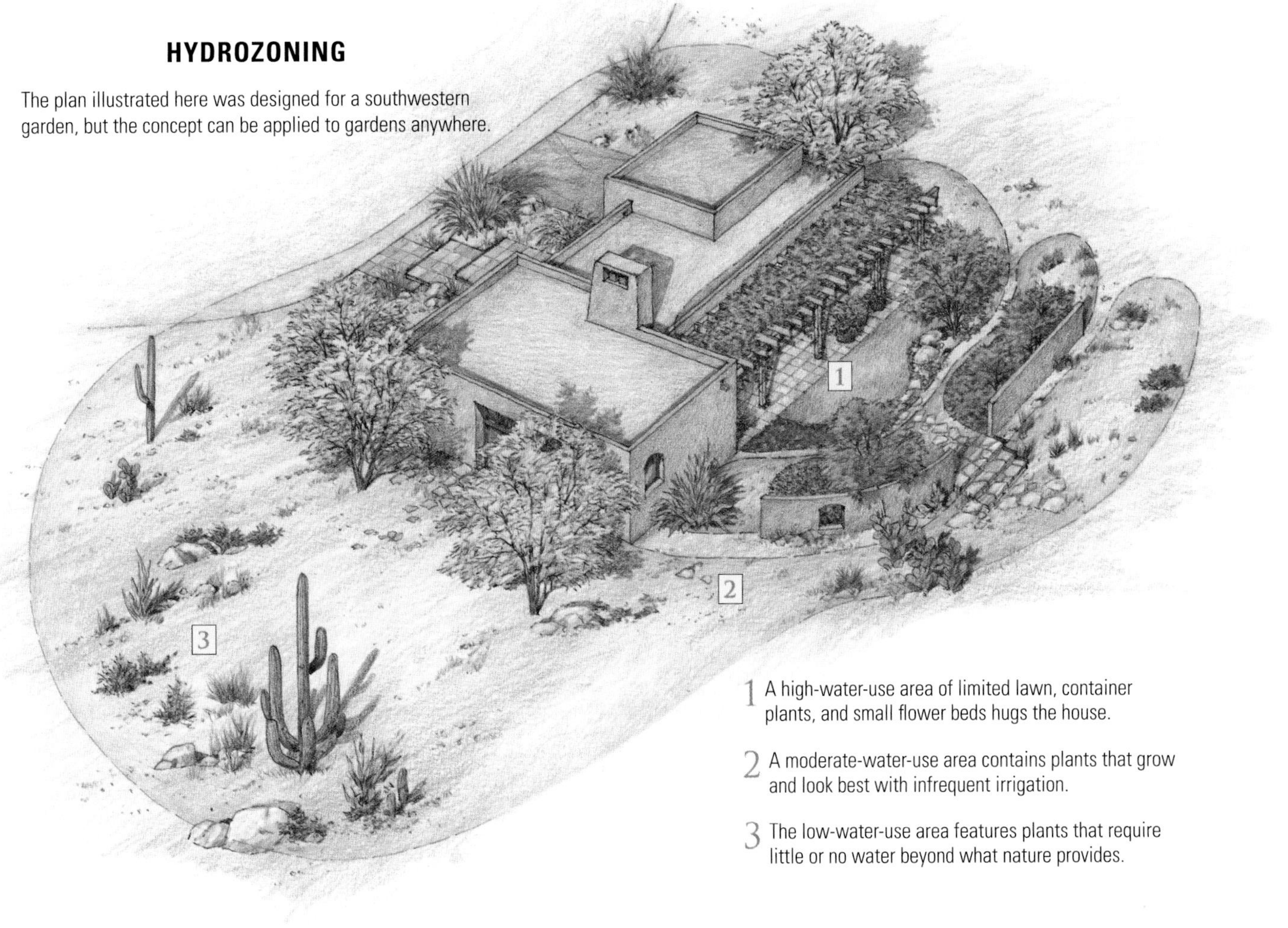

1 A high-water-use area of limited lawn, container plants, and small flower beds hugs the house.

2 A moderate-water-use area contains plants that grow and look best with infrequent irrigation.

3 The low-water-use area features plants that require little or no water beyond what nature provides.

But being a waterwise gardener doesn't mean you can't grow some plants that are less than ideally suited to your site and climate. Such plantings should be held to a minimum and placed where you can not only enjoy them but also most easily provide the extra care they demand.

Water-conscious gardeners will limit their lawn to a practical size (or even eliminate it, if they don't need one), apply garden water efficiently, improve the soil so that it retains moisture but also drains well, spread mulch around plantings to slow evaporation, faithfully remove weeds, and keep up with maintenance so that their gardens continue to be water conserving. On the following pages, these precepts are explained in more detail.

GROUPING PLANTS BY WATER NEEDS

Mixing plants that need little or no irrigation with ones that require regular moisture wastes water on the undemanding plants and can in fact damage them. You may even end up underwatering the thirsty plants to avoid overwatering the less thirsty ones. By organizing your yard into hydrozones—groups of plants with similar water needs—you'll simplify irrigation while giving your plants the amount of moisture they need for good health.

A practice originally developed for arid and semiarid climates, hydrozoning divides the landscape into zones of low, moderate, and high water use. Typically, high-water-use plants are located nearest the house and patio, with plants requiring less water progressively farther away. The great advantage of this scheme is that you don't have to drag hoses very far on a regular basis, nor extend an irrigation system to the outer reaches of a large yard. Also, if some of the most drought-tolerant plants look a little scruffy, it won't matter, because they'll be viewed mainly from afar.

The following are the hydrozones as originally conceived, though you don't have to stick to the three categories described. If you prefer, you can simply restrict plants needing regular water to one or several areas of the garden and select all water-conserving plants for the remainder of the landscape.

HIGH WATER USE. Here's where you put the thirstiest plants, the ones that get water whenever they need it—for example, lawns, annual flower beds, and vegetable gardens. In the arid Southwest even a small lush, high-water-use area can seem like an oasis; it is generally located on the north or east side of the house, where it can be enjoyed the most and where plantings

SOME UNTHIRSTY PLANTS

The following are some widely grown plants naturally equipped to prosper without regular water during the growing season. You'll probably find numerous others, many better adapted to your particular growing conditions. Check your local nurseries for drought-tolerant plants, especially ones native to your area or to similar climates.

Coreopsis

In these listings, ☼ means that the plant grows best in full sun, and ◐ means that it needs partial shade (that is, shade for half of the day or for at least several hours during the hottest part of the day).

TREES

☼◐ *Albizia julibrissin* (Silk tree)
☼◐ *Celtis* (Hackberry)
☼◐ *Elaeagnus angustifolia*
 (Russian olive)
☼ *Gymnocladus dioica*
 (Kentucky coffee tree)
☼ *Koelreuteria paniculata*
 (Goldenrain tree)
☼ *Lagerstroemia*
 (Crape myrtle)
☼ *Pistacia chinensis*
 (Chinese pistache)
☼ *Robinia* (Locust)
☼◐ *Sophora japonica*
 (Japanese pagoda tree)
☼ *Tilia tomentosa* (Silver linden)

TOP TO BOTTOM: *Lagerstroemia, Artemisia*

SHRUBS

☼◐ *Arbutus unedo* (Strawberry tree)
☼ *Artemisia*
☼◐ *Buddleia davidii* (Butterfly bush)
☼ *Callistemon* (Bottlebrush)
☼ *Caragana arborescens*
 (Siberian peashrub)
☼ *Caryopteris* (Bluebeard)
☼ *Cotinus coggygria* (Smoke tree)
☼ *Cotoneaster*
☼ *Lavandula* (Lavender)
☼◐ *Myrtus communis* (Myrtle)
☼ *Phlomis* (Jerusalem sage)
☼ *Pyracantha*
☼ *Rosmarinus officinalis* (Rosemary)
☼ *Santolina*

Cerastium tomentosum

GROUND COVERS

☼◐ *Aegopodium podagraria*
 (Bishop's weed)
☼◐ *Cerastium tomentosum*
 (Snow-in-summer)
☼◐ *Ceratostigma plumbaginoides*
 (Dwarf plumbago)
☼◐ *Cotoneaster*
☼◐ *Hypericum calycinum*
 (Creeping St. Johnswort)
☼ *Lantana*
☼ *Oenothera* (Evening primrose)
◐ *Potentilla neumanniana*
 (Spring cinquefoil)

Cosmos

PERENNIALS

☼ *Achillea* (Yarrow)
☼ *Asclepias tuberosa* (Butterfly weed)
☼ *Baptisia* (False indigo)
☼◐ *Centranthus ruber* (Red valerian)
☼ *Coreopsis*
☼◐ *Dietes* (Fortnight lily)
☼ *Echinacea purpurea*
 (Purple coneflower)
☼ *Gaura lindheimeri*
☼◐ *Iris* (Bearded iris)
☼◐ *Kniphofia* (Red-hot poker)
☼ *Liatris* (Gayfeather)
☼◐ *Potentilla* (Cinquefoil)
☼◐ *Sedum* (Stonecrop)
☼◐ *Stachys byzantina* (Lamb's ears)

ANNUALS

☼ *Celosia* (Cockscomb)
☼ *Cosmos*
☼ *Eschscholzia californica*
 (California poppy)
☼ *Gazania*
☼◐ *Gomphrena* (Globe amaranth)
☼ *Limonium sinuatum* (Statice)
☼ *Portulaca* (Rose moss)
☼ *Tithonia rotundifolia*
 (Mexican sunflower)

This traditional English border features tough, drought-tolerant perennials such as catmint *(Nepeta),* yarrow *(Achillea),* dwarf lavender, and penstemon.

will be least subject to water loss from wind and sun. Even in less extreme climates, this hydrozone is typically placed near the house or a much-used patio or deck for visual appeal and easy maintenance.

MODERATE WATER USE. Plants in this category need a bit more water than nature provides. Water them while they're becoming established—this may be as long as one or two full growing seasons—and during lengthy dry spells.

LOW WATER USE. These plants are irrigated only while they are getting established. Once they are well rooted, nature is their only source of moisture. This is a good hydrozone for hillsides—if you can avoid watering slopes, you'll prevent wasteful runoff.

CHOOSING DROUGHT-TOLERANT PLANTS

Depending on their evolutionary inheritance, some plants must have a lot of water to survive, whereas others perform well with less. The drier your summer climate, the wiser you'd be to favor naturally water-thrifty plants and to select as few as possible of the heavy water consumers. You'll find drought-tolerant species in every garden category: trees, shrubs, perennials, annuals, and so on (see the facing page).

Keep in mind that *drought tolerant* is a relative term, because the degree of dryness that a plant can tolerate also depends on the climate in which it grows. Some plants may be considered unthirsty in a relatively cool climate but not in a very hot one, or they may have a reputation for drought tolerance solely in areas that receive some summer rain. Also be aware that certain plants are drought tolerant only in shade but will need much more water in full sun.

The key is to seek out plants that will need little or no supplemental water given your own unique conditions. Because a plant's water needs reflect the conditions found in its native environment, for the least reliance on irrigation look to plants native to your area or to areas elsewhere in the world with a similar climate. These are the plants that not only survive but thrive on the moisture provided by nature.

You'll find that most drought-tolerant plants have physical characteristics that provide clues to their ability to withstand dry periods. Their leaf and sometimes stem surfaces may be hairy, sticky, or waxy to retain moisture. They may have fat, succulent

This planting of western natives—including flannel bush *(Fremontodendron),* California poppies, and Pacific Coast irises—needs little or no irrigation during the warm summer months.

THE RIGHT LAWN FOR YOUR CLIMATE

Climate should dictate your choice of lawn grass: cool-season grasses grow best in some areas, warm-season ones in others. If your water supply is sufficient (especially in areas where summer rain is usual), you can consider one of the high water consumers such as bluegrass, ryegrass, or St. Augustine grass, though a drought-tolerant grass will save water and give you a hedge against periodic drought. If you reside in an area with a scarce or unpredictable water supply, definitely select a water-conserving grass—even a native grass, if it thrives locally.

COOL-SEASON GRASSES. These grasses—including bent grass, bluegrass, fescue, and ryegrass—withstand winter cold but tend to languish in hot, dry summers. They remain an attractive green all year in mild-winter climates. Cool-season grasses are adapted to the Northeast, upper Southeast, upper Midwest, Northwest, cooler parts of California, and high-elevation areas that get some rain and aren't extremely hot in summer.

Once the traditional lawn grass, Kentucky bluegrass is being supplanted by the more drought-tolerant turf-type tall fescues. Though slightly coarser in texture than bluegrass, tall fescue makes an attractive lawn. The relatively new dwarf tall fescue varieties have the added advantage of lessening the amount of mowing required.

WARM-SEASON GRASSES. Unlike their cool-season counterparts, these grasses—including bahia, Bermuda, centipede, St. Augustine, and zoysia—grow vigorously during hot weather and go dormant in cool or cold winters. But even in their brown or straw-colored winter phase, they maintain a thick carpet. To keep them green in mild winters, you can overseed them with an annual cool-season grass. Warm-season grasses are grown in the Southeast, Southwest, lower Midwest, and hotter parts of California.

Bermuda and zoysia are among the most drought tolerant of the warm-season grasses. Because Bermuda grass tends to be invasive, it forms the best turf if not given too much water or fertilizer. Some of the newer zoysia varieties have a short dormant season and hence are brown for less time.

NATIVE GRASSES. Several drought-tolerant grasses are specialties of the Rocky Mountains and High Plains: blue grama grass, buffalo grass, and wheatgrass. Widely used in their native habitats, where they need only occasional to no irrigation or mowing, they are still being tested in other regions.

leaves that store water. Small-leafed plants can withstand drought better than large-leafed ones, because of their reduced leaf surface. Gray- or silver-leafed plants, too, are usually water conserving; the tiny hairs that give them their color also insulate them so that they retain water longer. Still other plants—notably many herbs—have aromatic oils that keep them from drying out.

Use good planting procedures to encourage the maximum drought tolerance of these plants. Set out plants or sow seeds at a time of year that will let the transplants or seedlings establish their root systems before the summer heat arrives. In mild-winter climates, fall is generally the best time to plant; in colder regions, wait until the ground warms in early spring. Choose small transplants: because of their smaller root system, they'll establish more rapidly and need less water initially than larger specimens, yet they'll catch up to or overtake the larger plants in a short time. Avoid very close spacing of plants—place them far enough apart so that their roots are not competing for the same soil moisture.

RE-EVALUATING THE LAWN

Most conventional lawn grasses use water at a rate disproportionate to the rest of the garden's needs, largely because they have a shallow root system that dries out quickly, especially in sandy soils.

Particularly in arid and semiarid regions of the West, where water conservation is a major concern, home gardeners are looking at lawns in a new light. They are reducing their lawns' size or even replacing them with plants that use less water; they're also seeking ways to water them more efficiently.

In the East, Midwest, and South, most lawns are watered only to supplement rainfall. How much irrigation is needed depends on

Limiting lawn size makes sense in regions where the grass must be irrigated regularly during the warm summer months.

THE PERIMETER-TO-AREA RATIO

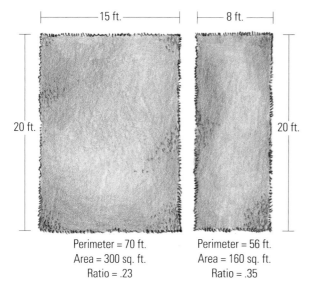

| 15 ft. | 8 ft. |

20 ft. — 20 ft.

Perimeter = 70 ft.
Area = 300 sq. ft.
Ratio = .23

Perimeter = 56 ft.
Area = 160 sq. ft.
Ratio = .35

A simple formula—dividing the perimeter by the square footage—will help you arrive at a lawn shape that lends itself to efficient watering by portable or underground sprinklers. When laying out your lawn, try not to exceed a ratio of .25.

the rainfall pattern, but few areas enjoy rainfall at regular enough intervals to take care of the lawn's total moisture needs. Thus, even in rainy-summer regions, knowledge and proper watering techniques are important to keep the grass healthy.

Looking at lawn from a practical standpoint makes sense in any climate. Consider how much lawn you really need, and whether you need one at all. If you want a lawn for kids' play, entertaining, or some other specific activity, limit the size to serve your purpose. Many landscape experts suggest that for most activities 600 to 800 square feet of lawn is plenty.

When planning a new lawn or modifying the one you have, keep the following water-saving guidelines in mind.

CHOOSE THE GRASS TYPE CAREFULLY. Look for the newer grass varieties that are attractive, tough, and less thirsty than traditional lawn grasses like Kentucky bluegrass. For tips on choosing a grass that is appropriate for your climate, see the opposite page.

If you're switching to a new lawn variety, you don't have to rip up the old lawn and replant or reseed. You can gradually acquire a new lawn by overseeding the existing lawn—if the new grass is available in seed. To overseed, rake the lawn vigorously with a metal rake and sow at 1½ times the recommended rate; then top-dress lightly with topsoil or screened compost. Keep the lawn well watered until new growth emerges.

PLACE THE LAWN WHERE IT WILL BE MOST USEFUL. If the backyard is the center of your activities, that's

SOIL POLYMERS

When added to soil, the tiny, gel-like particles called soil polymers will hold onto rainwater or irrigation water that would otherwise drain away. They are capable of absorbing hundreds of times their weight in water (though they soak up less in heavily fertilized or alkaline soil). They'll let you stretch the time between waterings and will help eliminate wide fluctuations of moisture between soakings.

The many brands are available in bags, boxes, and tubs. Some types are polymer based ("polymer" refers to the molecular structure), others starch based. The polymer-based types are longer lasting—up to 10 years or even longer—and more absorbent; they are widely used by nurseries and landscapers to retain soil moisture. In recent years they have become popular among home gardeners, especially those in dry climates or where dry spells occur frequently. For a true polymer, look for the term *cross-linked polyacrylamide* on the label. The less expensive starch-based products have been used chiefly in agriculture, as a soil amendment to temporarily improve the tilth of poor soil.

Incorporate the polymer evenly into the soil.

To be effective, polymers must be mixed into the soil—never simply applied to the surface. That's because the plants' root hairs must grow into the particles in order to extract water. Though the package directions may allow for pouring small amounts of polymer into holes you poke in the soil, adding water, and covering with soil, you'll get better results if you blend the polymer in evenly.

If mixed in at too high a ratio, the gel particles will ooze to the surface when it rains or when you add water. To get just the right mixture, you can hydrate the particles first. Soak the desired amount of polymer in water overnight; drain off excess water before blending the particles into the soil. Be sure to incorporate them at the recommended rate only: soil that stays too wet can kill your plants.

Soil polymers are most often used in container plantings; in fact, some potting mixes come with a polymer already incorporated. Although they can also be mixed into planting beds, only fairly small beds may be cost-effective to treat. To make the polymer go further, try to confine it to your plants' root level.

where the lawn belongs. If the front yard is never used, consider unthirsty ground covers or other plantings for it.

STICK TO LEVEL GROUND. Restrict turf to fairly level land, because water will quickly run off a sloping lawn. Mowing on an incline is also more difficult than on flat terrain.

CHOOSE AN EFFICIENT SHAPE. Design your lawn so that it's easy to water with portable or underground sprinklers. Very narrow side yards, for example, are hard to irrigate without throwing water onto your house or fence—or onto your neighbor's plants. Though curving or free-form lawns may be more appealing, squares and rectangles can be watered more accurately, with fewer sprinkler heads (if you have an underground system) and less wasted water.

To determine whether a particular shape is efficient, use this simple formula: divide the total perimeter of the lawn by its square footage. A perimeter-to-area ratio of up to .25 is considered efficient, anything higher inefficient. See the examples on page 15.

LOCATE PLANTING BEDS NEXT TO TURF. Even if you have a well-designed lawn, a little overspray from sprinklers may be difficult to avoid. Take advantage of this extra water by placing beds of thirsty annuals or vegetables next to turf, where they can profit from it.

KEEP UNTHIRSTY PLANTS OUT OF THE LAWN. Avoid placing low-water-use trees or shrubs in turf, as they will require less water than the lawn grass. You'll be overwatering them just to get adequate water to the lawn.

WATER TURF SEPARATELY FROM OTHER PLANTINGS. Lawns should be irrigated independently, because they must be watered more often and for briefer periods than other plantings. The proper duration will depend on the grass type, your general climate, and the current weather. For more on lawn watering, see page 98.

WATERING EFFICIENTLY

By enacting the principles of efficient irrigation, you'll not only prevent water waste but also avoid habitual over- and underwatering—practices that can damage or kill plants. As you will see, the system you choose and your management of it determine how efficiently you're watering.

When irrigation experts talk about efficiency, they are referring to the amount of water delivered to a plant's root zone compared with the amount that the plant needs for healthy growth. You play a major role in establishing this relationship, because the total-water-delivered factor is determined by how uniformly your chosen system distributes water and how long you run the

An underground sprinkler system is the usual way to water lawns in areas where rain can't be counted on to do the job. Though newer sprinklers are more water conserving than older types, a truly efficient system hinges on good design as well as proper operation and maintenance.

water. Even under the best circumstances, it's difficult to apply the exact amount of water that each plant needs, but keeping the concept in mind should help you avoid drastic overwatering. Don't skimp on water, though, thinking that you'll be more efficient—a plant will suffer if it doesn't get its minimum requirement.

The various irrigation systems used by home gardeners range from manual application with a hose or watering can to portable sprinklers and soaker hoses to fully automated drip and underground sprinkler systems. Your choice will depend on many factors, including your climate, the plants you're growing, the size of your landscape, and your budget. In a region that gets summer rain, you may get by nicely using garden hoses and soaker hoses for your vegetable and flower beds and portable sprinklers for lawn and ground covers. In a dry-summer area, you may opt to use a drip system for most plantings and a water-conserving underground sprinkler system for the lawn. The number of portable sprinklers and soaker hoses—or the size of a drip or underground sprinkler system—will depend on the size of your yard and your bank account.

You may decide to restrict your irrigation system to an area of high-water-use plants (see page 11) and to rely on drought-tolerant plants for the rest of the yard. To establish drought-tolerant plants in the most water-conserving way, plant them in fall or just before winter rains in mild-winter regions, in early spring in cold-winter climates. You may have to use the hose or watering can on these plants for several months, but that will be a temporary inconvenience.

Water from laser tubing (drip tubing containing laser-drilled slits along its length) soaks the root zone of these garlic plants.

Whatever irrigation method you use, apply water slowly enough so that it soaks in without running off. Unless you're flooding predetermined areas, such as basins or furrows, you'd be wise to regulate your watering with a timer, or controller. It's easy to apply too much or too little moisture if you just let the water run.

For detailed information on efficient water-delivery systems, see the chapter beginning on page 45. Figuring out when and how much to water is essential to efficient irrigation—see more about this in the chapter starting on page 89. To find out how best to water various plant types—for example, lawns, vegetable beds, and container plants—consult the chapter starting on page 97.

IMPROVING THE SOIL

You can improve any soil by incorporating organic matter such as compost, aged sawdust, or well-rotted manure. Adding organic material to clay soils opens up their tight pore spaces, improving drainage and allowing water to soak in rather than run off. Adding it to sandy soils fills some of the large air spaces, slowing the movement of water through the soil so you don't have to irrigate as often.

Amending your soil to a depth of about a foot, or as deep as is practical, produces other benefits. Your plants will have access to more moisture in a deep, loose soil than in a shallow or heavy one. It's better to amend an entire bed than just the backfill from the planting hole, because plant roots will tend to remain within the richer soil of the hole instead of moving out into the unamended native soil. Don't improve the soil, however, if you're growing native plants adapted to poor soil—just give them what they're used to.

Organic matter improves water absorption and drainage in clay soils; in sandy soils, it boosts water retention.

Even though you can't dig organic matter into a lawn, you can improve the soil supporting the lawn by leaving grass clippings in place after mowing—as they decompose, they'll filter into the soil. In existing planting beds, you can add organic matter in the form of a fine-textured mulch that will work its way into the soil over time.

As the organic matter decomposes, it provides plants with nutrients they need for healthy growth. This is a good way to feed your plants, especially if you want to avoid the moisture-demanding growth spurts produced by nitrogen-rich commercial fertilizers.

For more information on soils, see the chapter beginning on page 23.

SPREADING MULCH

One of the best things you can do for your garden is to apply mulch, a layer of insulating material placed on the soil surface. Mulch slows the rate of evaporation from the moist soil beneath, so mulched plants can go longer between waterings than those in bare soil. In hot weather a mulch also helps to moderate soil temperature, thus encouraging steady root growth.

In addition, a mulch minimizes erosion and gullying by dispersing the force of rainfall or irrigation water. Instead of forming channels in the bare earth and running off, the water seeps through the mulch and soaks into the ground beneath—a particular benefit on slopes.

Mulch also suppresses weed growth by effectively burying weed seeds and discouraging their germination. If any weeds do come up in the mulch, you can pull them easily due to the mulch's loose texture.

ORGANIC MULCHES. Traditional mulch is an organic material that breaks down over time and filters into the soil, improving the composition of the top few inches of soil and allowing water to penetrate more easily. Because it breaks down, it must be reapplied periodically.

Among the many organic materials you can use are bark (ground, shredded, or in chips) and homemade or commercially prepared compost. Agricultural by-products, typically sold where the product is grown, include ground corncobs, mushroom compost, apple or grape pomace, hulls from various nut crops, and cotton gin waste.

Under trees, you can simply allow fallen leaves or needles to become a natural mulch. However, avoid letting thin-textured foliage, such as maple leaves, accumulate;

TOP: A mulch of black plastic sheeting, which warms the soil in addition to conserving moisture and suppressing weeds, is ideal for heat-loving plants such as melons.

BOTTOM: Straw is a widely available organic mulch. It's virtually free of weed seeds, unlike the similar-looking hay.

when wet, it packs down into a sodden mass that repels water rather than allowing it to soak into the soil.

A layer of organic mulch should be 1 to 4 inches thick. (The coarser the material, the more generously it should be applied.) Spread the mulch under trees and shrubs, throughout flower and vegetable beds, and in containers. To conserve water, it's important to cover the plant's root zone. Keep organic mulches away from plant stems, because they can cause rot.

In cold-winter climates, mulch in late spring after the soil has warmed; spread too soon, mulch will delay warming and slow plant growth. Where winters are wet, mulch in autumn to help protect the soil during the rainy season.

INORGANIC MULCHES. These materials will conserve moisture, though they won't benefit the soil as organic materials do when they decompose. Rocks and gravel of various sizes and colors are the usual choices for inorganic mulches, which are used mainly in unplanted areas, rock gardens, and around native plants found naturally in rocky washes. Because these materials don't break down, they should be spread only as thick as needed for complete coverage.

Black plastic sheeting, sold in rolls, is sometimes used as a mulch between strawberries and other row crops. Lay strips of the plastic along either side of a row of plants, or cut or punch holes in it for each plant. Water applied from overhead will penetrate only where there is a gap or cut in the plastic. You can place drip lines beneath plastic mulch; for a better appearance, you may want to cover the sheeting with a thin layer of bark or rocks.

ELIMINATING WEEDS

Weeds are more than an unattractive nuisance in a waterwise garden—they compete with the more desirable plants around them for moisture. By getting rid of these pesky plants, you make more water available to the plants you want to grow.

It's impossible to banish weeds altogether from your garden, because weed seeds are carried by wind, birds and other animals, and muddy feet. Eternal vigilance is the key to curbing weeds. Immediately eliminate them—by hoeing, hand pulling, or applying an herbicide—before they produce seeds that will spawn an even larger crop the next year, or before their root systems spread out of control. Use a mulch to discourage weeds from returning.

KEEPING UP WITH MAINTENANCE

Any garden needs some upkeep if it is to be water conserving. Among your most important chores are maintaining your irrigation systems in good repair and getting to know your plants so you can tell if they are being adequately watered. You'll find that when it comes to fertilizing and pruning, less is more in a waterwise garden. And of course proper maintenance of your lawn—with a view toward making it more water efficient—is vital.

Continued on page 20>

MULCH MATH

A few simple calculations will enable you to assess the amount of mulch you need to cover any garden area. Mulches are usually sold in bags (by the cubic foot) and in bulk (by the cubic yard). Bags are practical for very small areas or for a few plants; you'll find bulk purchases to be more cost-effective for large-scale uses and to offer more choice of materials. Many nurseries and soil yards will deliver mulch to your front yard or driveway for an additional fee.

Whether you're buying bags or bulk, you must figure out how many cubic feet the mulch will cover when spread out. If you're buying in bulk, you then convert that number to cubic yards by dividing by 27 (there are 27 cubic feet to a cubic yard). Here are the steps:

1 Multiply length by width to determine the square footage of the area you want to cover. For example, 50 feet long by 10 feet wide equals 500 square feet. (For an odd-shaped area, break it down into squares and rectangles, figure the square footage of each, and total the results.)

2 Multiply the square footage by the desired depth of mulch to figure out how many cubic feet the mulch will occupy. If you want to cover your 500 square feet to a depth of 3 inches (3/12 or .25 foot), for example, multiply 500 by .25: you'll need 125 cubic feet.

3 In this example, it would save both work and money to buy in bulk. For example, to get 125 cubic feet of mulch, you'd need 63 bags in a 2-cubic-foot size (125 divided by 2) or 42 in a 3-cubic-foot size (125 divided by 3)! To order in bulk, you'd divide by 27 to get the number of cubic yards you needed (125 divided by 27 equals 4.6 cubic yards).

Clogged sprinklers not only waste water, but also can damage plants by depriving them of moisture.

MAINTAIN WATERING SYSTEMS. Inspect these conscientiously to be sure they're running properly. Repair leaky faucets or hose connections. On drip systems flush the filters, check all tubing for breaks (puddles, overly wet areas, or little geysers are clues), and look for clogged or broken emitters. Also lift the tubing while the system is operating, to be sure the emitters are actually dripping. On underground sprinkler systems, clean clogged sprinkler heads, replace broken sprinklers or risers, and adjust spray heads as needed if they're wetting pavement or patio. Also make sure that sprinklers are in the proper vertical position.

INSPECT YOUR PLANTS. Don't assume, just because your watering system is automated, that all is well with your plants. If you are irrigating dead or dying plants, you're wasting water. Tour your garden regularly to see how your plants are faring. Check with a soil probe as needed to see if moisture is getting to the full depth of the root system.

FERTILIZE ONLY AS NEEDED. Applications of fertilizer, especially those high in nitrogen, promote growth—which in turn creates a demand for more water. Fertilize as needed to maintain plant health, but don't overdo it. Vegetables and some annual flowers need regular feeding for good production, but don't strive for the largest tomatoes or zinnias if you want to conserve water. Fertilize your basic garden plants—trees, shrubs, vines, and perennials—when new growth is smaller than normal or its color is too pale. Withhold fertilizer from any plants that seem to be doing well without it.

In a water-conserving garden, you may prefer to rely on organic matter rather than commercial products for your plants' nutritional needs. Do this by periodically digging in compost or other organic material, and by applying organic mulches. You'll avoid the growth spurts—and accompanying water demand—caused by many commercial fertilizers.

PRUNE ONLY AS NEEDED. Most plants, when properly chosen to fit the allocated space, will need only occasional pruning to control wayward branches and to thin out superfluous or unproductive growth. Unless there's a reason to prune more radically, don't do it—heavy pruning stimulates vigorous new growth, which increases water demand.

MAINTAIN LAWNS PROPERLY. Good upkeep of turf is especially important, because the potential for water waste is so much greater than with other types of plantings. Mowing correctly and making the turf more penetrable are two easy ways to conserve water.

Mow to the proper height. Lawns that are cut too short dry out faster than those kept longer. Cut the lawn at the upper end of the recommended height range for that grass type (see the chart below). Grasses depend on a maximum blade surface exposure to capture the sun's energy for photosynthesis and to develop a more extensive root system, which will allow the lawn to go longer between waterings. The greater leaf area will also help conserve moisture and keep the soil cooler.

Rather than mow by the calendar, mow when the grass is about a third taller than the recommended height. Leave the clippings on the lawn; they'll decompose, returning organic matter and nutrients to the soil.

Dethatch and aerate. When water runs off lawns instead of soaking in, the cause may be either heavy thatch (an accumulation of dead grass stems, roots, and other debris) or soil compaction. Air and nutrients can't easily penetrate under these conditions, thus causing a decline in the lawn's health.

Some grasses are more prone to thatch buildup than others. The creeping grasses—most notably Bermuda grass, St. Augustine grass, bent grass, zoysia grass, and Kentucky bluegrass—develop thatch quickly. When thatch is excessively thick, you can feel a sponginess underfoot. At a more intermediate stage of development, thatch is sometimes difficult to recognize. Use a soil probe to extract a core of turf and roots a few inches deep, or pull apart material beneath the turf with your fingers or a hand trowel. Look for fibrous, corky material with roots growing in it but without the grit of the lower soil layer. If the thatch layer is shallow, remove it with a dethatching rake; rent a deeper-cutting flail reel or vertical cutter for layers more than 1 inch deep.

Aeration also helps air and nutrients penetrate the soil. Lawns subjected to heavy foot traffic or grown in clay soils can easily become compacted. Aerating them consists of punching holes through the surface. You can rent a motorized aerating machine or, for smaller spaces, use a simple pronged tool that you push into the soil as you would a shovel. Some garden supply companies sell aerating sandals—shoes with long spikes that you use to walk around on the lawn.

MAXIMUM AND MINIMUM MOWING HEIGHTS

Bahia grass	2–3 inches
Bent grass	¼–1 inch
Bermuda grass	1½–2 inches
Hybrid Bermuda grass	½–1 inch
Kentucky bluegrass	2–3 inches
Rough-stalked bluegrass	2–3 inches
Buffalo grass	2–5 inches
Fine fescue	1½–2½ inches
Hard fescue	1½–2½ inches
Tall fescue	2–3 inches
Perennial ryegrass	1½–2 inches
St. Augustine grass	2–3 inches
Zoysia grass	1–2 inches

A drip irrigation system can easily be added to even a mature, lush garden like this one. Snake the tubing through the plantings and position drip emitters over the plant root zones; then cover the tubing with mulch to make it practically invisible.

WISING UP AN ESTABLISHED GARDEN

If you already have a mature garden, you may not want to start over from scratch to make it more water conserving. Luckily, you can renovate it in stages—that way, you'll spread the work and the expense over several years, and you'll avoid disrupting the whole garden at once. Here's how to approach the task.

ASSESS WHAT'S THERE. Before making any changes, take a good look at what you already have. Note any weaknesses, such as drought-tolerant plants mixed in with heavy water consumers, and dry or soggy spots in the lawn after it's watered.

HYDROZONE YOUR GARDEN. Sketch on paper the existing planting areas, and mark any rearrangement you wish to make. You can then gradually uproot, transplant, or regroup to get plants of like water needs together. (Keep in mind that drip irrigation will allow you to be more flexible: you can bypass a drought-tolerant plant situated in an inappropriate hydrozone or add a thirsty plant to a drier hydrozone by extending drip tubing to it.)

TARGET AREAS FOR IMPROVEMENT. Depending on the extent of the changes you want to make, you may need to devise a long-range plan. Try to put your effort where you'll see the water-saving results first—for example, remove the few thirsty plants from an otherwise water-thrifty bed, or diminish your lawn in favor of a drought-tolerant ground cover.

REVIEW YOUR MAINTENANCE AND WATERING PRACTICES. A few simple changes can be made at the outset that involve little work or money but usually result in water savings. Here are some practical suggestions.

Mulch. Your flower and vegetable beds, especially, will benefit from mulch.

Weed. Get rid of moisture-stealing weeds as soon as they make an appearance.

Water carefully. You can often realize immediate savings in water use simply by repairing or upgrading an old, wasteful system or by refining your watering schedule to eliminate runoff. If you don't have a drip system, installing one—a fairly easy project for most home gardeners—will be a giant step toward good water management. And because drip systems are so easily expandable, you can start out small and lengthen the lines or add new ones on your own timetable.

Take care of turf. If you dethatch and aerate your lawn, water can seep down to the roots more easily, thus promoting healthy, deep roots.

TOP: Check your lawn for thatch—a buildup of dead stems, roots, and other debris that impedes the penetration of water. Some thatch is normal, as in this bent grass lawn.

BOTTOM: To get rid of thatch more than an inch thick, rent a flail reel or vertical cutter.

WATER, SOIL, AND PLANTS

When you irrigate, you're not applying moisture directly to plants, even if you're spraying them with a hose or sprinkler. Instead, you are watering the soil. You'll have a better understanding of irrigation if you digest some basic facts about the ways in which water, soil, and plants interact with one another.

A plant's survival depends on water, which it obtains from small pores in the soil. However, not all soils are alike. The type of soil you have—its texture and structure—determines whether water soaks in easily or puddles up and runs off, how deeply it penetrates, and how well it is retained. You must therefore take the characteristics of your particular soil into account when you irrigate.

Knowing how water behaves in the soil will also help you irrigate effectively. When you saturate your soil, some of the water quickly drains away, but the rest is held in the soil by a gravity-defying force called capillary action. This moisture gradually dissipates as the plant absorbs it and as it evaporates from the soil surface. You must replenish that moisture before it's too late: the drier the soil becomes, the harder it is for plants to absorb the remaining water and the greater the danger of permanent wilting.

Healthy plants need water and air, both of which are supplied by the soil.

Plants like this apple tree that are grown for their edible fruit produce tastier, more bountiful crops when given ample water.

WHY WATER?

Why *do* gardeners take care to water their plants during dry weather? You may do it because you've noticed that your plants wilt when they don't receive enough moisture, or that they stop growing or slack off in fruit or flower production. But exactly what role does water play in plant life?

Water is the lifeblood of plants. It not only keeps them plumped up and erect, but it's an essential ingredient in various physical and chemical processes taking place within them. Water also transports mineral nutrients into plants, which can only take them up in solution.

JUST PASSING THROUGH

Plants absorb water and the dissolved minerals it carries from the soil primarily through their root hairs. The solution enters the *xylem*, a sort of one-way pipeline that conducts them upward and distributes them throughout the plant.

More than 90 percent of the water that travels up the pipeline exits the plant through its leaf surfaces in the form of water vapor. This process of water loss through the leaves is called *transpiration*. In addition to cooling the plant, it exerts a "pulling" force on the water in the pipeline, which keeps it moving from the soil up through the plant and into the leaves.

Minute pores in the leaves, called *stomata* (from the Greek *stoma*, or mouth) regulate transpiration by opening and closing. Normally they're open during the daytime, when the plant is engaged in *photosynthesis*—a process unique to plants whereby they manufacture their own food. In addition to letting water vapor escape, the open stomata allow carbon dioxide from the atmosphere to enter the leaves. Thus, both substances needed for photosynthesis—water and carbon dioxide—are present in the leaves. The plant converts these molecules, in the presence of sunlight, into a simple sugar. That sugar, again in a water solution, moves downward from the leaves to the roots in another one-way pipeline called the *phloem*. If any part of the plant along the water and sugar pipelines—roots, stem, branches, or leaves—is injured, this finely tuned system will be impaired, perhaps beyond recovery.

The stomata of most plants close at night, when cooler conditions prevail and plants demand less water; they don't need to take in carbon dioxide then either, because sunlight, a key ingredient of photosynthesis, is absent. Stomata also close during the day whenever the sky is heavily overcast or a dark cloud passes overhead, as well as whenever the plant is stressed by extremely hot or cold temperatures.

Even when the stomata are open, weather affects the rate at which a plant transpires. It slows down on dull, windless, or cool days. On windy or hot, dry days plants lose water more rapidly—a point may even be reached when the roots can't get

TRANSPIRATION

Water enters a plant through its root hairs, travels upward to the leaves, and escapes as water vapor through the leaf pores.

water from the soil as fast as they need it, and the plant wilts. (It may recover when the sun sets and the stomata close.)

Plants transpire a great deal of water—much more than you might guess. For example, 2 to 4 quarts of water will pass through a single corn plant on a hot summer day. Larger plants transpire even more water—in the case of a mature birch tree, about 20 to 100 gallons a day during the growing season.

Does that mean you have to replace all of the transpired water every day, even if it's 100 gallons? You might—if the plants are growing in containers, in a very dry soil, or in a porous soil with little groundwater. But many soils retain much of the required moisture between rainstorms and irrigations. In some cases, plants can tap into plentiful groundwater stored in the soil. So your soil conditions determine when you should start replenishing transpired moisture as well as the amount you should apply. (See the discussion of soils beginning on page 26.)

AVOIDING EXTREMES

Your goal in watering is to ensure that your plants get an adequate supply of water for their needs—neither too much nor too little. Plants tend to be healthier when they have access to a fairly constant level of moisture, rather than being subjected to cycles of very wet and very dry conditions.

OVERWATERING. Bog plants thrive in constantly wet soil, but most plants languish and may die in those conditions. Waterlogged soil contains plenty of water but few or no air spaces, which provide plant roots with needed oxygen. In such cases you may observe some roots that have concentrated just under or above the soil surface, where the soil dries faster and oxygen is more available. Roots cut off from the air supply decay and thus cannot take up water or mineral nutrients.

Besides this root rot, other symptoms of habitual overwatering are slow, stunted, or weak growth. Normally green leaves become greenish yellow, water-soaked spots or pale green blisters form on leaves and stems, and fruit cracks. Often gardeners think that an overwatered plant's poor appearance is due to lack of water, so they apply more moisture and thereby worsen the situation.

UNDERWATERING. A plant's root hairs will dry out and die in soil that is overly dry for that particular plant. Those suffering from a mild water deficiency are usually slow growing and stunted, just as they are when overwatered. Under long-term water stress, plants may permanently wilt or stop growing. Other symptoms are diminished crops and discolored leaves, flower buds, and flowers; underwatered plants are also more susceptible to pest damage. Drought-stressed plants may eventually die.

Even if you manage to avoid these extremes when irrigating your garden, remember that you don't apply water in a vacuum; the soil your plants are growing in also plays a major part in your calculations.

TOP: Most plants suffer when they are overwatered. Allow the soil—especially a clay soil—to dry partially between irrigations, so that air can get into it.

BOTTOM: This plant's wilted, discolored foliage is a sign of underwatering. A drought-stricken plant may not recover when the moisture level is increased, but give it time to recuperate before declaring it a goner.

SOIL PARTICLES

CLAY
Less than ¹⁄₁₂,₅₀₀ in.

SILT
Up to ¹⁄₅₀₀ in.

FINE SAND
Up to ¹⁄₂₅₀ in.

MEDIUM SAND
Up to ¹⁄₅₀ in.

LARGEST SAND PARTICLES
¹⁄₁₂ in.

SOIL TYPES

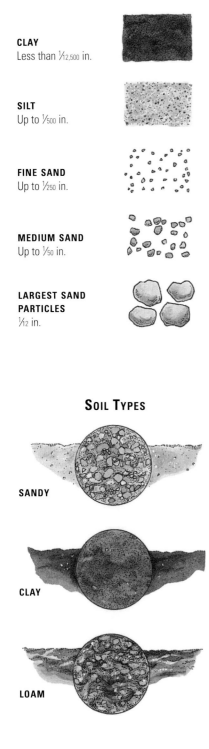

SANDY

CLAY

LOAM

UNDERSTANDING SOIL

Unless you're growing your plants hydroponically (in a nutrient solution instead of soil), you must take your soil into account when you irrigate. After all, this substance—whether you call it dirt, earth, or soil—is where plant roots grow and where they get most of the raw materials essential to their development.

If you've ever gardened in different regions, or maybe even in different neighborhoods of a single city, you may have encountered vastly different soils. Perhaps the topsoil in one garden was several feet deep and a pleasure to dig, whereas in another it was barely a spade's length deep and hard as a rock.

Although these two soils may seem to have little in common, in fact they and all other garden soils contain the same ingredients: mineral particles, living and dead organic matter, and pore spaces for water and air. But proportion is everything. A good garden soil is made up of approximately 45 percent minerals, 5 percent organic matter, and 50 percent pore space. Such a soil will have a good balance of small and large pores; water is attracted to the small pores but drains out of the large ones, which then fill with air. Thus, plants growing in good soil will have plenty of access to water and oxygen.

SOIL COMPONENTS

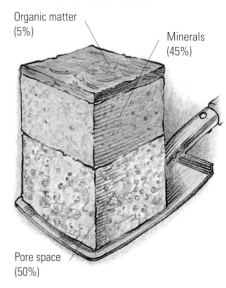

Organic matter (5%)

Minerals (45%)

Pore space (50%)

The proportion of large and small pores is not always ideal, however. Dense soils, with many small pores, can hold a lot of water but not much air. Loose soils, with a preponderance of large pores, are well aerated but can't retain moisture for long.

The type of soil you have, then, determines the availability of water and oxygen to your plants. It also governs how easily water penetrates the soil and how long it stays there, and thus will influence the way you irrigate—how often you water, the amount of water you apply, and the irrigation method you choose. The following discussions of texture (mineral content and particle size) and structure (the arrangement of particles) will help you become familiar with your soil.

SOIL TEXTURE

Soil scientists classify the many soil types strictly by their mineral content—the percentage by weight of sand, silt, and clay that the soil contains—without taking organic matter or pore space into consideration.

The 12 soil classes include pure clay, sand, and silt as well as sandy clay, sandy clay loam, sandy loam, loamy sand, silt loam, silty clay loam, silty clay, clay loam, and loam. The soils are categorized by the particle type or types that predominate.

Loam, often referred to as the ideal garden soil, has the characteristics of the three basics—sand, silt, and clay—but none overshadows the others. If your soil has somewhat more sand, it's called sandy loam. An increase in clay changes loam to a clay loam, an increase in silt to a silt loam, and so on. You can feel some of these differences for yourself when working your soil (see "What Do You Have?" on page 28).

Sometimes other minerals found in a soil will modify the soil's official designation. For example, a sandy loam containing more than 20 percent gravel is called a gravelly sandy loam. Generally though, only sand, silt, and clay are figured into the classification. The main difference among the three is particle size (see the illustration of soil particles on the opposite page). Sand particles, which are graded from very coarse to very fine, are the largest. The finest grains of sand are still larger than silt particles, which require magnification to see. The even smaller clay particles can be viewed only with an electron microscope.

Sand and silt are basically broken-down rock. Clay, in contrast, consists of particles that have undergone a chemical change and so differ from the rock from which they originated. Most soils contain a mixture of all three minerals: loam, for example, consists of roughly 40 percent sand, 40 percent silt, and 20 percent clay.

TEXTURAL TRAITS. The dominant particle in your soil gives it certain characteristics that you should be aware of when you irrigate. Some of these are good, but others are not so good.

Keep in mind that you can't do anything about the texture of your soil, short of hauling in new soil. If your soil is sandy, that's its nature. If it has more clay particles than sand or silt, your soil is clayey. However, amending the soil can improve it in many ways; see "Soil Structure" on page 29.

Note, too, that some soils change textures at different depths. For example, a layer of clay under a sandy soil or loam can restrict drainage and keep the upper level unusually wet. (See the illustration of stratified soil on page 28.)

Sandy soil. This "light" soil has large pores, so water enters easily and moves through the soil quickly, leaving the soil well aerated. But because the particles are also large, the total surface area for holding water is less than in soils with smaller particles (see below). This means that you must water sandy soil frequently during dry weather. Overwatering a sandy soil doesn't result in runoff or plant damage but rather in waste—water and nutrients will quickly wash down below the plants' root zone, where they do no good.

Clay soil. A soil high in clay contains tiny, flattened, platelike particles that pack closely together, leaving little pore space for either water or air. Often referred to as "heavy" soil, clay absorbs water slowly and causes it to puddle quickly and run off. Once

HOW DEEP DOES WATER GO?

Soil texture determines how deep water will go in a soil. If you were to evenly apply the same amount of water to the following soil types, you would find that it penetrates about three times deeper in sandy than in clay soils. The following figures show approximately how deep 1 inch of water will go.

Sandy soil	12 inches
Loam	7 inches
Clay soil	4–5 inches

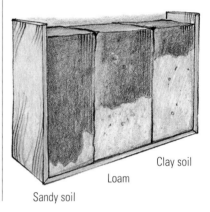

Clay soil

Loam

Sandy soil

WATER-HOLDING CAPACITY

To understand the difference in water-holding capacity between clay and sandy soils, visualize the 2-foot cube at right as one sand particle and the eight 1-foot cubes at left as clay particles. (In reality, there would be many more clay cubes, but we've shown eight for clarity.) The single sand cube has the same outside dimensions as the smaller clay cubes placed together—but the little cubes have a total of 48 square feet of surface to which water can adhere, whereas the large cube has only 24 square feet of surface.

AVOIDING SOFTENED WATER

If you have hard water—so called for its excessive levels of dissolved minerals (mainly calcium and magnesium but also iron and manganese)—you may be softening it to prevent it from rusting your pipes and other household items with which it comes into contact.

Softened water is fine for household use, but it's damaging in the garden. It's the softening process that causes the trouble—most softeners work by chemically exchanging sodium in the form of rock salt for the "hard" minerals. That sodium, released in the landscape, will build up in the soil and destroy its structure.

Some softeners exchange potassium in the form of potassium chloride for those minerals. Though this form of salt is not as bad for the soil or for plants as the sodium in rock salt, unsoftened water is still preferable in the garden.

To avoid problems, use hose bibbs that bypass your water-softening system. If you have a permanent irrigation system, be sure it taps into your main water-supply pipe at a point before the softener does. If you have a septic system and have been advised not to direct the backflush from the softener into it, be careful where on your property you do dispose of it, to avoid harming plants.

---

wet, however, clay soil retains water well. Plants growing in clay can go longer between waterings than those in other soil types. If you don't keep that in mind, you can easily overwater them.

Silty soil. This category really describes silt loam, because pure silt soil is uncommon. The soil contains mostly small pores; thus, water is more available than air is. Like clay, silty soil holds water well, so you can go longer between irrigations.

Loam. Though loam contains a mix of all three particle types, none predominates. It has all the advantages of sandy, clay, and silty soils, yet it has none of the drawbacks. With its good balance between large and small particles, loam is easy to wet, dries out at a moderate rate, and is well aerated—which earns it its reputation as the ideal garden soil.

WHAT DO YOU HAVE? Your soil texture may be obvious to you, or you may have heard your neighbors complaining about their heavy clay soil or perhaps extolling the virtues of their sandy loam. If you're uncertain of your soil type, you can have a sample analyzed at a soils laboratory (this is particularly advisable if you suspect you have a problem soil). On the other hand, by following the steps below you can make a fairly good guess at your texture simply by feeling it.

You can learn a lot about your soil's texture just by handling it in various ways.

- Take about a tablespoon of soil from a point at least several inches below the soil surface; add just enough water to moisten it (use distilled water if your tap water is high in minerals) and let it soak for a minute or so. Rub your thumb over the sample. A gritty or scratchy feeling will tell you that the soil has a high sand content. A sample that feels slippery but not sticky indicates silt. A soil high in clay will feel both slippery and sticky. Loam will feel neither particularly gritty nor especially smooth.

- Now try to roll the sample into a pencil shape. If it crumbles before getting thin, it's low in clay. If the soil is very clayey, however, you should end up with a pencil about 3 inches long that holds its shape. If the pencil forms but then breaks, you probably have clay loam.

- Finally, squeeze the soil between your thumb and forefinger and try to make a ribbon of it. A clay soil will easily ooze out in ribbons. A silty loam may ribbon slightly before breaking.

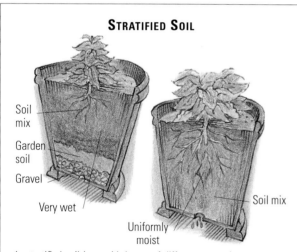

STRATIFIED SOIL

Soil mix

Garden soil

Gravel

Very wet

Soil mix

Uniformly moist

In stratified soil (one with layers of different texture), water must saturate one layer of soil before it moves to the next lower layer. This is why you should incorporate materials thoroughly when you amend your garden soil and avoid layering gravel or other materials in container plantings. If you just lay topsoil over a different soil type without mixing it in, water is likely to go as far as the boundary between the types and then just pool or flow away to the side.

SOIL STRUCTURE

Though you can't change the texture of your soil, you can improve it by modifying its structure—that is, by changing the physical arrangement of the soil particles. Sand and silt consist of individual grains, whereas clay particles form aggregates. In a well-structured soil the three kinds of particles gather in clusters: clay aggregates with sand and silt trapped between. Soil scientists refer to this ideal as a crumb structure.

If you lack good soil structure, the best way to create it is to add organic matter such as homemade compost, well-rotted manure, or leaf mold. Humus—the soft, usually dark substance left when organic matter breaks down—acts as a glue to keep the particle crumbs together.

Adding organic matter to this vegetable bed will improve the soil's structure.

Though you might be tempted to improve a tight clay soil by adding sand, the regrettable result would be concrete. Instead, work in lots of organic matter. It will break up the tightly packed clay particles and create more pores, so that the soil will absorb water more easily and hold more air. The spaces will also improve drainage and allow plant roots to grow deeper than they otherwise would. Organic matter has a similar effect on silty soils, creating larger pores and improving their aeration and drainage. In sandy soils, humus lodges in the already-large pore spaces, slowing the flow of water and enabling the soil to remain moist longer.

Unfortunately, you can't build up a large reservoir of organic matter in your soil, because it continuously decomposes, consumed by organisms within the soil. (This happens at a faster rate in hot climates than cool ones.) You must therefore keep adding it over time. In steamy climates like those found in the Deep South, amendments disappear so quickly that they're practical only for areas that are worked regularly, such as vegetable gardens or annual flower beds.

Another way to create larger aggregates in clay soil is to add calcium, which is attracted to the clay particles and, like humus, acts as a glue. You can incorporate this mineral in the form of gypsum (calcium sulfate).

Remember, just as you can build soil structure, you can also destroy it. Avoid anything that compacts the soil—for example, running heavy equipment over it or even walking repeatedly over the same area. Don't till or dig when the soil is wet; let it dry out until it's barely moist before working it. Too much sodium in the soil also destroys structure—a good reason to avoid irrigating with softened water (see the facing page).

Another caution: some plants will lag in improved soil. Native plants, especially, are better off with the type of soil they are accustomed to in nature—if their preference is for heavy clay, that's what they should get.

Working manure into this tight clay soil will help create more pore space.

TESTING YOUR DRAINAGE

Good drainage (neither too slow nor too fast) is crucial to the healthy growth of most plants. You may have noticed that "needs good drainage" is a common qualification in many plant encyclopedia listings. Plants native to dry regions, such as lavender, are especially sensitive to excess water in their root zone. You can grow these plants in rainier climates, however, as long as your soil drains very well.

To check your soil's drainage, dig a 2-foot-deep hole and fill it with water. After it drains, fill it again. If it hasn't completely drained in 48 hours, your soil probably has a serious drainage problem. The solution is to drill through the obstruction with a soil auger, install drainage tiles, or plant in raised beds.

Gardeners in many parts of the arid West must contend with such impediments as hardpans and salty soils.

A DRAINAGE CHIMNEY

Purchased soil

Drainage chimney

Topsoil

Porous soil

Hardpan

If a hardpan is close enough to the soil surface to interfere with plant growth and impede drainage, you can form a "chimney," or narrow passage, to porous soil underneath it. A jackhammer may be necessary to break through a thick layer of soil.

Raised beds offer a way to circumvent the problem of poor drainage. Water may puddle in the native soil, but it has no difficulty flowing through the imported soil, where plant roots are growing.

PROBLEM SOILS

Some soils present obstacles to watering. These include soils that have a hard layer or are compacted, as well as ones with an excessive salt content. Most of these problem soils are found in dry climates of the West.

HARDPAN. As the name implies, a hardpan is an impervious layer of soil. In the case of caliche, a common type of hardpan in the Southwest, the layer consists of lime. Hardpans usually form in regions that receive just enough rain to dissolve minerals and carry them a few inches below the soil surface, but not enough to leach them out. After decades of this process, the minerals cement the soil at that level into a hard layer. The closer the hardpan is to the surface, the more trouble it causes: it prevents water from draining and keeps plant roots shallow.

Penetrating a hardpan, even a thin one, can be difficult. If you can't break through with an iron bar or soil auger, landscape professionals can sometimes help with special equipment. Rather than break up the whole pan, you may prefer to have them create a drainage "chimney" through it at the base of each planting hole (see the illustration).

Thick hardpans may require the installation of subsurface drainage, a project usually handled by a landscape contractor. As an alternative, you can resign yourself to planting in raised beds or on mounds.

COMPACTED SOIL. At new homesites, heavy construction equipment can seriously compact the soil, leaving few pores in it for water or air to enter and limiting drainage. Special soil-loosening equipment capable of ripping the soil to a depth of 18 inches or so may remedy the situation. This, too, is a job best left to a landscape contractor.

SALTY SOIL. This condition is common near the seashore and in arid climates, especially in valleys. It can also be found where fertilizers and manures have been overused. The problem is that excess salt in the soil interferes with the ability of most plants to take up water.

You can eliminate many kinds of salts by periodically leaching the soil, thus washing the salts below your plants' root zones. If the excess salt in question is sodium, how-

ever, it actually bonds to the soil particles and can't just be washed away. By incorporating gypsum (calcium sulfate), you can displace the sodium with calcium. You must then irrigate well to leach out the dislodged sodium.

Experts can often look at the whitish salt crust on a soil and tell whether it is sodium or another salt, but most home gardeners would have to send a sample to a soils laboratory for identification. If you don't want to do that, you can just add gypsum before leaching, to cover both possibilities. With any kind of excess salt problem, obviously, pouring on salty water would be counterproductive—if your local water is high in salts and you don't get enough rain to leach the soil, you may have to settle for growing salt-tolerant plants.

HOW WATER BEHAVES IN SOIL

Understanding how plants use water and knowing your soil type are both important pieces of the irrigation puzzle—but you also need to know something about how water moves about within the soil, and the intricate relationship between the two elements.

If gravity were the only force in effect when water entered the soil, all the water would simply drain away, leaving none for the plants. Fortunately, soil has a force to counteract gravity: *capillary action.* (This is the same force that makes water rise in capillary tubes—though there the attraction is between water and glass, here between water and soil particles.) To explain this and other complex interactions, we'll make use of the same terminology that soil scientists employ.

When the soil is *saturated*, all pore spaces are filled with water. The roots of most plants will start to die if left in saturated soil for 24 hours. However, gravity pulls most of this moisture downward, below the root zone.

Once this *free water,* or gravitational water, has drained away the soil is said to be at *field capacity.* The free water has actually drained from the larger pores, which then become filled with air. The water remaining in the soil is held in the smaller pores and in a film around each particle; this is called *capillary water* because it is held there by capillary action.

Capillary water is the moisture that plants absorb and use for their growth. How much of this water is present in a soil at field capacity depends on the soil type—more water will be held in a clay soil than a sandy one, for example, because of its more numerous small pores, greater particle surface area (see the illustration on page 27), and particularly strong attraction for water.

Capillary water leaves the soil gradually in two ways: by evaporation from the soil surface and by transpiration from the plant (see page 24). Knowing the rate at which this water dissipates can benefit you as a gardener, because then you will know how much water to replace. In many localities, Cooperative Extension offices and water companies provide residents with figures on local *evapotranspiration*—a combination of evaporation and transpiration—to help them figure out when to irrigate their lawns; see page 94 for more information. (Other figures developed for uniform commercial crops don't apply to a home garden's mixed plantings.)

Plants readily absorb water from soil that is at or near field capacity, but as the soil dries out the film of water around each soil particle becomes thinner and increasingly difficult for plants to absorb. If the soil is allowed to become too dry, the plant won't be able to pull out sufficient water fast enough to replace transpired water. When that happens, the plant wilts. It may droop during the day but perk up at night, when the transpiration rate slows; at some point, however, it won't be able to recover even at night unless it is watered. If it isn't, the wilting will become permanent, and the plant won't recuperate even if you pour on gallons of water.

UP, DOWN, AND SIDEWAYS

You may think of water as moving only in one direction, but it actually flows through the soil pores in various directions. Water moves downward after a rain or irrigation. It moves upward when it evaporates from the soil surface and when it is taken up by plant roots. Water also moves horizontally, though not as much in sandy soils or potting soils— a fact you must take into account when using drip emitters. (You'll need a greater number of emitters, or more closely spaced emitters, in very porous soils.)

Plants in containers are more prone to wilting than are the same kinds of plants in the ground, because their smaller amount of soil dries out faster.

WATER
SOURCES

Your source of garden water—whether a municipal water main, a private or shared well, a pond, or reclaimed household water—will influence your type of irrigation setup and some of the components you use.

If you're on a municipal system, you'll usually have enough water for lawn sprinklers (though perhaps not the kind requiring the most pressure) and drip lines. But before you head to the hardware store or order sprinkler parts from a catalog, you should know how much water is available to you for garden use, and at what pressure that water is delivered. This chapter explains how to gather the information you'll need to plan a system that works properly. You'll use these data in the next chapter, when you proceed to the specifics of design and installation.

In rural areas, wells feed pumped water to sprinkler and drip lines. If you're fortunate enough to have a pond, lake, or other body of water on your property, you may be able to tap into it for garden use. Rainwater, whether stored for later use or channeled to plants during storms, is a clean, free source. Gray water—reclaimed water from certain household drains—is another free source, though not a clean one. Properly collected and distributed, however, it's safe to use on most plants and around people.

This serene pond does double duty as a source of irrigation water for a lucky rural resident.

MUNICIPAL WATER

Most people watering their gardens are drawing from a domestic water supply provided by their city, town, or other municipality. The water is piped to individual properties, where typically it is metered and the property owner charged according to the amount of water consumed.

If you're in this situation, you just turn on the tap to get water whenever you want it—as long as you pay the bills to keep the water flowing. The supplier takes care of the water quality, though you may choose to add filtration or other purification equipment.

Usually the water is delivered at a suitable pressure and flow rate to run an irrigation system. Before installing one, however, you should determine your specific water pressure and flow, because those key aspects of water delivery will influence pipe size, your choice of irrigation heads, and the number of separate irrigation lines you'll need. Begin the planning process by ascertaining the size of your water meter and service line, and then by actually measuring your pressure and flow.

YOUR WATER METER

In regions where the ground doesn't freeze deeply, the water meter can usually be found in a box similar to this one.

In mild-winter regions, the water meter is usually located in a concrete box in the ground near the front of the property, at the edge of the sidewalk, or in the parking strip. Where the ground freezes, the meter is generally protected in the basement.

A municipality supplies area homes with a set size of water meter. The two most common residential water meter sizes are ⅝ inch and ¾ inch; some newer properties may have 1-inch meters. You should know the size of your meter, because it determines how much water can flow from the city main into your service line at any given time. The larger the meter is, the more water can pass through it. The size is usually stamped on the side of the meter, and it may also be listed on your water bill. If it's not, your supplier can provide this information.

Because changing the size and location of a water meter is usually expensive, most people work with what they have. For a fee, most water companies will install a second meter strictly for irrigation—something you may want to consider if your existing meter is too small to supply your household needs and also run more than a couple of lawn sprinklers at a time.

YOUR SERVICE LINE

The water supply pipe from your water company's main to your house is your service line. Most newer homes have a copper or polyvinyl chloride (PVC) service line. Older homes are often served by galvanized steel, a material that clogs over time, constricting the amount of water that can flow through the pipe.

Use the string method to figure out the diameter of your service line (see the box on the opposite page). You may have to excavate to gain access to the pipe—try digging next to the water meter, on the side closest to your house. If you're not sure where the meter is located, or if it's embedded in a large paved area, look for the pipe at the point where it enters the house.

UNDERSTANDING WATER PRESSURE

You may not give much thought to water pressure—the force exerted by water—if the stream from your faucet or garden hose is strong enough for your needs. But if you're planning to install an irrigation system, you'll have to know more precisely how much pressure is available to you.

The various types of sprinkler heads and drip emitters are designed to work within a certain pressure range. You may discover that you have enough pressure for sprinkler spray heads but not for rotary heads (rotors), which throw water farther and need considerably more pressure to operate properly. On the other hand, because a drip system works at much lower pressure than conventional sprinklers do, you may have to reduce your pressure on drip circuits.

Water pressure is technically defined as the force exerted downward by a column of water. It's expressed in pounds per square inch (psi) because it is measured in terms of its weight at the bottom of a 1- by 1-inch column. Here's a key statistic to remember about water pressure: a 1-foot-high column of water exerts .433 psi at its base. That means water gains .433 psi for every vertical foot of elevation drop, and it loses .433 psi for every vertical foot of elevation rise. This is true for water as it travels from its source to your service line as well as while it courses through irrigation pipes in your landscape.

Instead of pumping water to their customers, many municipal water companies rely on gravity, or the downward force of water due to its weight, to move it. In hilly areas, such as many parts of the West, water reservoirs are located near hilltops. In regions with flat terrain—much of the Midwest, for example—water is pumped up into storage towers to create enough pressure to propel the water under its own weight through city mains. Because water gains pressure as it runs downhill, the farther below the water source you live, the higher your water pressure will be.

If there were a difference of 150 feet in elevation between the water level in a reservoir or water tower and your outdoor faucet, the resulting pressure created would be 65 psi (multiply 150 by .433 psi). If your faucet were only 90 feet below the water supply, the pressure would be 39 psi (multiply 90 by .433 psi).

There are two kinds of pressure to consider: static and dynamic. Static pressure is the amount of water force measured in a closed piping system, when the water is not moving. The size of your water meter or service line has no bearing on static pressure—the determining factor is either the height of the water source or the power of a pump. Dynamic pressure is the amount of force measured when the water is flowing. As you'll see, the dynamic measurement is affected by all of the components of a pipe system through which the water travels, including the water meter and service line.

ELEVATION AND WATER PRESSURE

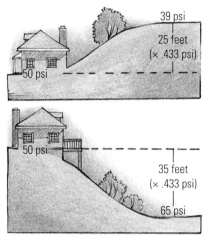

Water is delivered to both houses shown above at 50 psi. But water traveling through irrigation pipes to their backyard gardens will lose pressure in the case of the upslope garden (top) and gain pressure in the case of the downslope garden (bottom).

In flatlands, water is often stored in towers something like this one to create sufficient pressure for local water users.

SERVICE LINE SIZE

Determine the diameter of your service line by wrapping a string around the pipe, using a pen to mark the two points that overlap, and measuring the marked length. All numbers shown below are in inches.

APPROXIMATE STRING LENGTH	2³/₄	3¹/₄	3¹/₂	4¹/₈	4³/₈	5¹/₄
Size of copper pipe	¾		1		1¼	
Size of PVC pipe		¾		1		1¼
Size of galvanized steel pipe		¾		1		1¼

STATIC PRESSURE

Typical static pressure—remember, this is the force of water in a *nonflowing* pipe system—from a city water main is around 60 psi, but readings throughout North America range from about 30 psi to well over 100 psi. You can call your local water supplier or fire department to get an estimate of the static pressure in your neighborhood, but the numbers can vary within a single block. You'll get a more specific reading if you take your own.

An inexpensive pressure gauge will do the trick. Irrigation suppliers, home-improvement centers, hardware stores, and tool equipment companies usually sell them. Some irrigation suppliers may lend you such a gauge—or a combination pressure and flow gauge that measures not only water pressure but also flow rate (see page 38).

Measure your static water pressure at an outside faucet (hose bibb)—the only difference among the readings at different faucets would be due to elevation changes or to a pressure regulator or booster pump connected to a particular faucet. Make sure no other water is running inside or outside the house while you are taking the reading. Attach the pressure gauge to the faucet; turn on the faucet all the way and note the pressure. Depending on water consumption in the neighborhood, pressure can fluctuate, so take several readings throughout the day. Consider your static pressure to be the lowest number you obtain.

If you're using a combination pressure and flow gauge, keep the flow part closed while you take the static pressure reading.

The gauge indicates static pressure (in this case, 38 psi).

DYNAMIC PRESSURE

If your static pressure is 50 psi, or perhaps 70 psi, don't imagine that all that force is at your disposal for your irrigation system. Rather, you will be working with dynamic pressure—the force of water in a *flowing* pipe system.

Because water loses force as it travels, dynamic pressure isn't as easily calculated as static pressure is. Keeping in mind that water loses .433 psi for every vertical foot of elevation gain, you can see that you'll forfeit pressure when running irrigation pipes uphill. Another type of pressure loss isn't as obvious: water loses pressure through friction, as it rubs against the interior walls of pipes, valves, fittings, and other irrigation components.

Friction losses are higher as the length of the pipe run increases, when the interior of the pipe is very rough, as you add more heads and other elements, and as the water speed increases. As you can imagine, the farther from the water source an individual sprinkler or emitter is, the less pressure is available to operate it. In an underground sprinkler system, there can easily be a pressure loss of 20 to 25 psi from the water meter to the farthest sprinkler. That's significant, considering that many sprinklers are designed to work best at 30 to 50 psi. If you start off with marginal pressure for some types of sprinklers, you may not have enough force for the head to operate efficiently once the water gets there.

Generally, the farther that a sprinkler throws water, the greater the pressure needed to operate it. Conventional spray-head sprinklers that throw water in a radius of only 8 or 10 feet will work best at approximately 30 psi. Most rotor sprinklers throwing water long distances (a radius of 40 feet or so) will need about 40 to 50 psi to function properly. Also, a certain amount of pressure (it varies among manufacturers) is required to push up a pop-up head.

To see what happens when water is flowing, leave the pressure gauge on the faucet after taking the static pressure reading, and open another outdoor faucet. Watch the needle on the gauge dip. The reading you get at this point won't necessarily be

Your water pressure may be the determining factor in your choice of sprinklers for an underground system. Rotors (top) typically operate at a higher pressure than do spray heads (bottom).

TOO HIGH? TOO LOW?

If your pressure is too high for the type of irrigation system you want, or if it's causing sprinkler heads to mist or fog, you can easily fix the problem. Either a pressure regulator for your entire system or individual pressure-reducing valves will restrain the force to a suitable level—and also reduce wear on your equipment.

Low water pressure (30 psi or less) is a problem in some areas, such as Long Island. Once the water travels through pipes and fittings, its pressure is reduced even further, making lawn sprinklers unthinkable unless the pressure is raised. Installing a booster pump in your irrigation main line will increase the pressure enough to accommodate rotors and other high-pressure sprinkler heads. For efficiency's sake, you can wire a switch called a pump-start relay to the sprinkler circuits needing high pressure; it will activate the pump only when valves operating those circuits turn on. Any drip circuits will work at the normal low pressure.

RECOMMENDED PIPE SIZES

Using the appropriate size of pipe for your flow rate (see page 38) will help keep friction, and thus pressure loss, to a minimum. These size recommendations also provide for water to move at a safe speed. Don't use a smaller-diameter pipe size than indicated, though you can choose a larger one—in fact, sizing up can help compensate for low static pressure or very long pipe runs. In the chart at right, find the pipe material you plan to use and

PVC pipe is available in many different diameters.

the flow rate you've measured; at the bottom of that column you'll see the appropriate pipe size.

PIPE MATERIAL	MAXIMUM FLOW RATE (GPM)				
PVC Schedule 40 (irrigation mains and lateral lines)	up to 4	5–9	10–13	14–23	24–32
PVC Class 200 (lateral lines only)	up to 5*	6–10	11–17	18–27	28–36
Polyethylene pipe	up to 4	5–9	10–13	14–23	24–32
Copper Type L	up to 4	5–7	8–12	13–21	22–30
RECOMMENDED PIPE SIZE	½"	¾"	1"	1¼"	1½"

*Use Class 315, the lightest-weight ½-inch PVC pipe commonly available.

the same as on your planned irrigation system, because different pipes and components will be involved, but it will give you an idea of what to expect.

Irrigation professionals address the problem of pressure loss mainly by choosing pipe of a sufficiently large diameter for the system. Not only does water encounter less resistance as it runs through properly sized pipes, but it travels at a relatively low speed. Water speed is a function of the amount of water trying to get through the pipe relative to the pipe's diameter—meaning that the same amount of water travels faster through a small pipe than a larger one. Fast-moving water may sound like a good idea, but it's not. The greater the speed, the more turbulence (and hence friction) and the more pressure loss. Also, "water hammer"—pipes rattling when rapidly moving water hits a closed valve—becomes a problem.

The experts often start with the static pressure reading as a baseline, and then account for pressure losses along the entire path of the irrigation system by consulting a series of friction loss charts—there are separate ones for all the various pipe and valve types and sizes. Being exact is important for the pros, because for economic reasons they're trying to use the smallest-diameter pipe or valve that will operate properly in the situation.

You don't have to be as exacting to construct a good home irrigation system. You'll be in good shape if you're aware that dynamic pressure is always lower than static pressure and that there are steps you can take to limit friction loss. The most important step is to use the recommended pipe size (see the chart above). Also, try not to overload your system with overly long pipe runs or too many components—if necessary, break a large irrigation circuit into smaller ones to avoid this.

FIGURING OUT FLOW

Besides identifying your water pressure, you'll need to calculate how much water travels through your pipes, to ascertain whether your supply line can accommodate the irrigation system you want. Flow rate—the amount of water that moves through pipes in a given period—can be measured in either gallons per minute (gpm) or gallons per hour (gph). Your flow rate determines how much water you can have spraying or dripping at one time.

All types of irrigation heads and emitters have designated output rates (expressed in gpm or gph), so it's a matter of assigning only as many of those devices to a given circuit as your water supply can handle. (Note that you won't be able to mix different types of devices, such as spray heads and rotors or sprinklers and drippers, on the same circuit and still get good performance.)

The lower your flow rate, the greater the number of independent irrigation circuits you'll need, especially if you're using conventional sprinklers. Flow isn't as critical a factor for drip irrigation, because comparatively little water is dispensed.

Remember, flow is different from pressure, the force propelling the water. It's possible to have high static pressure but low flow—perhaps as a result of narrow-diameter or corroded pipes. Flow tends to be especially restricted in old galvanized steel supply lines, which are coated with rust-resistant zinc on the exterior but highly susceptible to corrosion on the interior; eventually, they may carry only a fraction of the water intended. Connecting your irrigation pipes as close as possible to the beginning of your service line is important in such cases, to avoid the corroded pipe.

HOW MUCH WATER?

Take a flow reading at the outdoor faucet closest to where your service line enters the house. You'll probably get a conservative number if the hose bibb is some distance from the beginning of the line and the pipes are even slightly corroded. You can take your reading at another faucet if you intend to tap into that faucet.

If you're planning to cut into the service line to connect your irrigation pipes, the outdoor faucet must be the same diameter as the service line to give you a realistic reading. (If it isn't, instead use the chart below to estimate flow.) You don't have to worry about size differences if you intend to hook your irrigation system directly to the faucet.

You can measure the rate at which water is flowing in one of two ways: with a flow gauge or a bucket test. The chart below gives flow rates through an uncorroded service line; you may want to compare the reading you take with the figure indicated on that chart.

FLOW GAUGE. After attaching the gauge to the faucet, turn on the faucet all the way. Then slowly open the gauge all the way and note the reading on the flow dial.

Professionals often use both parts of the combination gauge together to see if there is adequate flow and pressure for the system they have in mind. After taking the static pressure, they slowly open the flow section, which causes the needle of the pressure dial to dip. They continue to open the gauge until the pressure reads at the level needed to operate the irrigation heads they want. Then they can see the available flow at that pressure.

BUCKET TEST. Place a bucket of known capacity under the faucet. With a stopwatch, count the seconds it takes for water from the fully open faucet to fill the bucket to that point. To determine the flow rate in gallons per minute, divide 60 by the number of seconds you recorded; then multiply by the bucket's capacity in gallons. For example, if a 1-gallon bucket fills in 5 seconds, the flow rate is 12 gpm (60 divided by 5, multiplied by 1); if a 5-gallon bucket fills in 30 seconds, the flow rate is 10 gpm (60 divided by 30, multiplied by 5). To get a gallons-per-hour rate, which is useful in planning drip systems, multiply your gpm total by 60.

TOP: This gauge serves a dual purpose: it records flow (gpm) on the lefthand dial and pressure (psi) on the righthand one.

BOTTOM: A bucket test is an alternative, low-tech way to determine flow.

FLOW RATES AT A GLANCE

This chart offers a quick way to determine your approximate flow rate, based on your water meter size, service line size, and static water pressure reading. It's always a good idea, though, to conduct your own flow test—closest to where you'll tap into your service line or at the faucet to which you plan to connect your system.

The flow figures here indicate your entire household water capacity in gallons per minute. The rule of thumb is to use only up to 75 percent of that capacity for irrigation, so that you'll have water available in the house. (However, don't use a lot of water indoors while your irrigation system is running—even if your capacity allows it, you may not have enough pressure for the system to work properly.)

STATIC PRESSURE (PSI)		30	40	50	60	70	80
WATER METER	SERVICE LINE*	FLOW RATE (GPM)					
⅝ inch	½ inch	2	4	5	6	7	7
	¾ inch	4	7	9	10	10	12
	1 inch	5	8	11	13	15	15
¾ inch	¾ inch	4	8	11	13	15	15
	1 inch	7	11	15	17	17	17
	1¼ inches	9	14	18	20	22	22
1 inch	¾ inch	5	9	10	10	10	10
	1 inch	8	14	17	17	17	17
	1¼ inches	11	20	24	24	24	24

* Based on 50-foot, uncorroded Schedule 40 PVC service line. Deduct 2 gpm for copper pipe. Corrosion inside a galvanized steel service line will skew these figures; measure the flow at a faucet as described in the text above.

PROTECTING AGAINST BACKFLOW

Most municipalities require that irrigation systems include a backflow prevention device, to avoid contaminating the potable water supply. Even if you can't envision your irrigation water flowing backward, it can happen. For example, if you were applying fertilizer through a hose-end sprayer when a sudden drop in pressure occurred in the city water main, the fertilizer might be siphoned into the city pipes. Various types of backflow preventers are available, so check with your building department to find out what's required locally.

Antisiphon valves, also called vacuum breakers, are a frequently used device. They create an air gap at a high point in the irrigation system that prevents water from being sucked back into the city supply. An antisiphon valve and the control valve that regulates flow to an irrigation circuit are often combined in a single unit that may cost little more than a control valve alone. (You can also buy a small antisiphon device that screws onto a hose bibb—use it alone, to protect the household water supply, or as the backflow preventer for a small drip system that attaches to the bibb.)

A simple vacuum breaker screws onto the faucet.

Two main types of antisiphon valves are common in home irrigation systems: atmospheric and pressure.

The atmospheric vacuum breaker is the least expensive backflow preventer. Because it operates by gravity, it can be used only in lines that aren't under constant pressure. Install one in each circuit, after the control valve and before the irrigation heads, making sure that you position the device at least 12 inches higher than the highest head on the circuit.

There's no problem with putting the more expensive pressure vacuum breaker on a line that remains under pressure, because it is spring loaded and doesn't rely on gravity to shut it down. It is installed in the irrigation main pipe, before the control valves; it must be at least 12 inches above the highest head on the system.

An antisiphon valve combines a backflow preventer with a control valve.

Another device is the double check-valve assembly, which is installed at the beginning of the irrigation system. It doesn't have to be higher than pipes or heads, as it is not affected by elevation differences. But because it doesn't show any sign when it fails, many municipal codes don't allow it. Instead, they require the costlier reduced-pressure assembly, which is also installed at the head of the system. Aboveground installation is typical, though some locales allow burial in a pit.

CHOOSING A POINT OF CONNECTION

One of your first decisions will be where to start your irrigation system. It may be at an outside faucet, in your service line somewhere between the meter and the house, or—in a freezing climate—at the basement meter. Typically, far fewer laws govern irrigation systems than indoor plumbing systems, but consult your local building department about any restrictions or permit requirements.

If you have good flow at a faucet, the easiest course of action is to make the connection at the pipe serving that faucet. (In the case of a small drip system, you won't even have to remove the faucet to insert a tee—just screw the components onto the hose bibb.) Tapping in at that location means less trenching, because you'll probably want to locate your valve manifold—a grouping of control valves—near the house for easy access and to keep them out of harm's way.

Screwing drip system components onto a faucet is the simplest type of connection.

However, if the flow at the faucet is restricted by a corroded galvanized steel supply line or a small-diameter pipe leading to the faucet, cutting into your service line makes more sense—particularly for a conventional sprinkler system. Cutting in as close as possible to the beginning of the service line will give you access to water before it starts losing pressure and flow. (If tapping into your service line is at all restricted in your area, you may have to tie into a faucet, even if flow and pressure are reduced there. Keep in mind that this will be perfectly adequate for a low-pressure, low-volume drip system, in any case.)

The idea of severing your main water supply may intimidate you, especially if you're not sure you'll be able to restore service to the house. In most cases, however, a compression tee does a quick job of putting PVC, copper, or galvanized steel pipe back together—it slides right over the cut ends of the pipe and seals each with a rubber gasket and compression nut. (Some experts advise against using a compression tee in the basement; ask your irrigation or plumbing supplier about other options.) You may want to call in a professional if you don't have access to your main water shutoff, or if you simply prefer to have someone else make the connection.

For specifics on hooking up to your house water supply, see page 54.

OTHER SOURCES OF WATER

If you get your domestic water from a well instead of from a municipal water main, for better or worse you are your own water company—you're responsible for water quality as well as maintenance of the water supply. As long as the flow from your well is sufficient, you should be able to tap into it for irrigation.

If you have a body of water on your property, you may be able to draw from it for all or part of your irrigation needs. Additional sources for irrigation, bound to appeal to avid recyclers, include rainwater and reclaimed household water.

WATER QUALITY

Before irrigating with water drawn from a private source, be sure it's appropriate for plants and poses no health threat to humans. You may want to have it analyzed at a laboratory. (Remember, you're not looking for drinking quality in non-well water, just irrigation suitability.)

The water should always be filtered to remove algae, sand, and other materials that would clog irrigation components. Filtration is especially important for drip systems: whereas a standard filter will suffice for relatively clean municipal water, a larger or more elaborate filter may be necessary for water from a well, pond, or other body of water. Be sure to clean the filter frequently.

Although filtration can take care of many problems, it won't have any effect on hard minerals (calcium, magnesium, iron, or manganese), iron slime bacteria, and other contaminants that come out of solution only when exposed to air. If your water contains high levels of hard minerals, do yourself a favor by choosing irrigation heads and emitters designed to clog the least, and maintain them conscientiously.

You'll want to protect your well or other body of water by including a backflow prevention device in your irrigation system; the various types are described on page 39.

WELLS

You may have your own well, or you may share one with neighbors. In either case, you probably have records of flow rate and other tests conducted when the well was dug or drilled. When you purchased the property, you may have arranged for additional testing.

If you don't have any records, you can measure your flow rate in the same way that you would for a municipal water source—with a flow gauge or bucket test (see page 38). You can do this at either an outdoor faucet or the wellhead. Be sure to run the water long enough so that the pump comes on and stays on before you take your flow measurement.

If you have low flow (less than 10 gpm), buying a larger pump won't increase your output. However, a water storage tank should provide you with ample water for both household and irrigation needs. If low pressure is a problem (you can put a pressure gauge on the wellhead pipe to get a reading), you may have to replace your well pump with a more powerful one or install a booster pump.

Inform yourself about the quality of your well water—for example, whether it contains hard minerals—before choosing irrigation components. If you soften it for household use, be sure to tap into your pipes at a point before the softener device (see page 28). The salts in softened water will harm most plants as well as destroy your soil structure.

The various kinds of wells include fairly shallow dug types (top) and deeper drilled ones (bottom).

Chlorinated well water can still be used for irrigation if the chlorine is in small enough concentrations (fewer than approximately 200 parts per million). Low levels won't harm most plants, but chloride remaining on the leaves of salt-sensitive plants after the water evaporates can cause leaf burning. To avoid this damage, apply water to the soil instead of on the plants. If you must sprinkle, do so at night, when water evaporates more slowly and the plant can absorb the chloride in solution.

Well water can be a very reliable source of irrigation water, but keep in mind that even deep drilled wells have been known to run low—or even dry—during long, hot

A large natural pond so close to a property's lawn and garden areas is an ideal source of irrigation water.

rainless spells. If your well's capacity drops significantly, be prepared to cut back on irrigation. With a shared well, you'd be wise to set up a watering schedule with your neighbors to avoid placing too great a strain on your common resource. Even when a well contains ample water, it can still put out only a certain number of gallons per minute.

SURFACE SOURCES

You may want to tap into a pond, lake, stream, creek, or river if one lies close enough to the area that will be irrigated—and if its water quality is acceptable (see the opposite page).

If the source lies entirely on your property, you can probably draw from it as desired, unless an agreement gives neighbors certain water rights. In most areas you are allowed to use water that touches your property, though the amount you're permitted to take may be set down in writing or may be informally agreed upon by neighboring property owners. If you're not sure of your water rights, consult your local water district, water control board, or other authority.

Unless the water is elevated above your garden, allowing you to move it by gravity, you'll need a pump. Keeping the pump from sitting on the muddy, silty, or sandy bottom will help protect it from clogging. Suspend it, if the water is deep enough; otherwise, you can encase it in a homemade screen box fash-

ioned from scrap lumber and wire mesh. In moving water (streams, creeks, and rivers), weigh down the box to anchor it. If pump performance starts to erode, check the protective box and the pump intake for any clogging.

COLLECTED RAINWATER

Harvested rain provides a clean, free supply of water for irrigating plants. It's a particularly good source for seedlings, orchids, and other plants that may be sensitive to the chemicals and salts found in some wells and municipal water supplies. You can collect the water at any time of year in which rain falls, even during winter, and save it for warm weather, when plants are thirsty.

Just a few inches of rain are enough to provide thousands of gallons of runoff from an average-size roof, so the amount of water that you can collect is limited only by the size of your containers. If you have room for a big holding tank, consider one that keeps a low profile in the landscape.

A easier, cheaper option is a garbage can system that you put together yourself using 30- to 35-gallon, heavy-duty plastic trash containers; ready-made rain barrels are also sold. You can buy linking kits to connect two or more barrels, thus increasing your storage capacity. Both homemade and purchased systems capture water from downspouts. If a downspout is too low, or situated where you can't conveniently put a barrel, you can reroute it by adding elbow and extension pieces.

Position your barrel where there's adequate drainage to handle spillover. In warm climates, protect barrel-stored water from excessive heat buildup by keeping it in shade. A screen over the top will keep leaves from washing or blowing in and fouling the water. Add a few drops of vegetable oil to discourage mosquitos from breeding in it.

You can get water out of homemade systems in a number of ways: dip it out with a bucket, suction it out with a hose, pump it out with a small submersible pump, or add a spigot (manufactured barrels come with one).

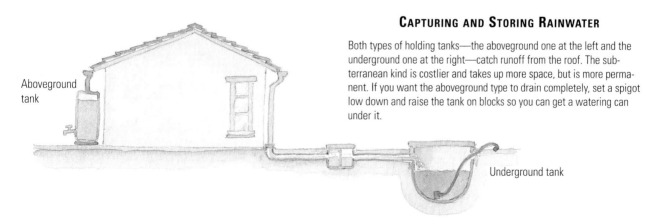

Aboveground tank

CAPTURING AND STORING RAINWATER

Both types of holding tanks—the aboveground one at the left and the underground one at the right—catch runoff from the roof. The subterranean kind is costlier and takes up more space, but is more permanent. If you want the aboveground type to drain completely, set a spigot low down and raise the tank on blocks so you can get a watering can under it.

Underground tank

This manmade rock wash collects runoff from the roof, slows its flow, and channels it to the plants that need irrigation the most.

DIRECTING RAINFALL

Collecting rainwater can be an anytime-it-rains activity, but directing the rain to plants is most useful during the warm summer months, when plants need it the most. A system of routing water to plants is practical in any region that receives some summer rain—especially if it comes in deluges that would otherwise run off.

In all summer-rainfall regions, you can build simple soil basins around plants or dig furrows between rows of them to capture rainfall. In some of the driest parts of the Southwest, many home gardeners mimic nature by recreating desert washes: they channel rainfall from the roof through downspouts and along the washes to planting areas.

Additionally, some gardeners in the Southwest are reviving the ancient system of sunken gardens. The technique consists of excavating planting areas to catch rain as well as to protect plants from drying wind and extreme heat. Ideal for the arid Southwest, where relatively small amounts of rain come in brief torrents, sunken gardens can also be effective in other regions where summer downpours are common.

There are no hard-and-fast rules for constructing such gardens. In some cases, the beds are large (perhaps 20 by 30 feet) and dug to a depth of 5 feet; topsoil is blended with organic matter and returned to the hole, so that the finished soil level is about 2½ feet below grade. A raised, 2-foot-high earthen berm all the way around the hole, shaped from the remaining excavated soil, completes the construction.

Another design, shown below, calls for a series of smaller beds (about 4 by 5 feet) excavated to a depth of 1½ to 2 feet, with amended topsoil bringing the soil level up to just slightly below grade. Leftover soil is formed into hard-packed berms only a few inches high, which double as walkways between the beds.

This sunken garden consists of beds excavated a couple of feet and then filled with amended soil to just below grade level. Excess soil is mounded around the edges.

GRAY WATER

Water reclaimed from shower, bathtub, bathroom sink, and washing machine drains can also be used to irrigate plants. Be aware, however, that not all household water is suitable for reuse. Much of the water from dishwashers and kitchen sinks is contaminated with grease and food particles and should not be used. Toilet waste water, called black water, should never be collected.

Most residences produce 20 to 40 gallons of gray water per person each day, so this source has the potential to cut municipal water or well use dramatically. Gray-water systems are now legal in many localities, including throughout the state of California. You'll probably need a permit to make permanent plumbing modifications, so consult your local building authority before constructing your system.

PRECAUTIONS FOR USE

The health risks from gray water are minimal if you gather and apply it properly. Never collect washing machine drainage contaminated by soiled diapers, the clothing of people with infectious diseases, or cloth used in poultry or wild game preparation. Nor should you use greasy, soapy water full of suspended solids.

Don't collect gray water after washing strong chemicals (such as products for opening clogged drains and those containing boron, chlorine, or sodium) down the sink. Water that has run through a water softener is likewise unsuitable. Of the standard laundry detergents, liquid ones contain less sodium than powdered ones do, and those labeled biodegradable are usually the least harmful. Most plants will not be affected by mild soaps or shampoos.

COLLECTING GRAY WATER

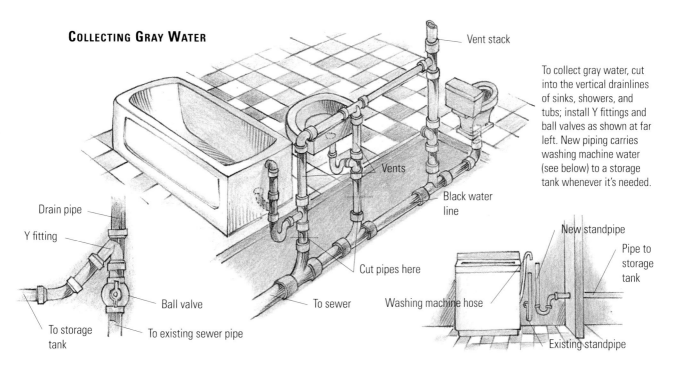

To collect gray water, cut into the vertical drainlines of sinks, showers, and tubs; install Y fittings and ball valves as shown at far left. New piping carries washing machine water (see below) to a storage tank whenever it's needed.

Labels on illustration: Vent stack · Vents · Black water line · Drain pipe · Y fitting · Ball valve · To storage tank · To existing sewer pipe · Cut pipes here · To sewer · New standpipe · Pipe to storage tank · Washing machine hose · Existing standpipe

PLANT DOS AND DON'TS

Gray water is suitable for all types of plantings except those whose soil is reworked throughout the season, such as vegetable gardens and annual flower beds. Also avoid applying gray water to any plant whose edible part is near or below the soil surface.

Shade-loving plants native to forested areas where acid soils predominate won't thrive on gray water. That's because the sodium, potassium, and calcium in detergents—a typical constituent of gray water—are alkaline, and thus tend to raise the soil pH. Acid lovers to keep away from gray water include azaleas, rhododendrons, bleeding hearts, camellias, gardenias, foxgloves, hydrangeas, primroses, violets, impatiens, ferns, and begonias.

Also avoid using gray water on seedlings as well as on salt-intolerant plants such as holly, crape myrtle, star jasmine, and redwoods.

COLLECTING GRAY WATER

A simple system that needs little or no plumbing know-how consists of a submersible pump placed in a full bathtub and hooked to a hose that goes out the bathroom window to a collection barrel, or even directly to a planting area (wait for the water to cool off, though, before pumping it to plants). You can also direct the outflow from your washing machine's drain hose to a collection barrel, which must sit at a lower level if the water is to move by gravity.

More sophisticated systems typically involve cutting into the drainpipes of some plumbing fixtures and diverting the gray water through new pipes to a storage tank, where it's filtered and stored for up to a day. To collect water from main plumbing lines, the pipes must be accessible from a crawlspace or basement. (See the illustration above.)

Ideally, the storage tank should be located above the planting areas, so that water can be distributed by gravity. If it isn't, you'll have to install a sump pump. To screen out hair and large particles in the gray water, make a shallow basket from ¼-inch hardware cloth and hang it inside the tank, just below the rim. Provide handles so that you can lift it out frequently for cleaning.

DISTRIBUTING GRAY WATER

The safest way to apply gray water is below the soil surface or under several inches of mulch. Below-surface applications eliminate human contact, and the soil filters out any harmful organisms.

A good distribution method is through a mini–leach field. An easy way to construct one is to bury 10-foot lengths of 3- or 4-inch-diameter perforated drainpipe in a shallow trench; there should be about 2 to 3 inches of gravel under the pipe and about 6 to 8 inches over it. Glue a sweep 90° fitting (ask at any plumbing- or irrigation-supply store) on each end and attach a short length of pipe to bring each one above ground; cap these stubs. Put in one of these 10-foot-long systems wherever you intend to deliver gray water. When you're ready to water, remove one cap, insert the hose leading from the storage tank, and open the valve or turn on the pump. Simply move the hose from one system to the next to complete watering.

You can also hook the storage tank to a drip system, as long as the system uses emitters and not microsprays. You can even water your lawn this way, with an underground drip system (see page 81). Additional filtering is critical when using gray water in a drip system in order to keep the emitters from clogging: place a filter on the tank inlet (old nylon stockings will do the trick) and use a 200-mesh drip-irrigation filter at the outlet.

Exactly what kind of watering setup should you have? The choices range from simple tools for applying water manually to sophisticated options such as an underground sprinkler

WATERING
SYSTEMS

system wired to a timer. Your decision depends on your climate, the category of plants you're growing, the size of your yard, your water supply, the amount of time you're willing to devote to irrigation, and your budget.

The simpler the method of irrigation, the more laborious and time-consuming your role in its operation will be. Toting watering cans or hauling hoses isn't so bad, though, if you only have to do it occasionally, when nature fails to provide rain.

If you can't depend on nature, you'll appreciate an automated drip or underground sprinkler system. It will require more up-front effort and expense, especially for large landscapes, but the installed system can run while you're doing something else (such as sleeping) and it won't demand any heavy labor of you. If the system is to work efficiently, though, you will have to maintain it properly and pay close attention to your watering schedules.

Before deciding on a particular system, see the chapter beginning on page 97, which recommends the best watering methods for some common types of plantings.

Each of these raised beds is watered by two parallel emitter lines.

KEEPING IT SIMPLE

Simplicity may be the operative word if you live in a rainy-summer climate, especially if you have just a few individual plantings to water during dry spells. A permanent irrigation system may be overkill when watering cans, garden hoses, hose-end nozzles, portable sprinklers, and soaker hoses will serve nicely. You should have no trouble finding a good selection of these simple watering tools at local nurseries, garden centers, home-improvement and building centers, and hardware stores, as well as through mail-order companies.

It's not always a simple task to remember how long a hose or portable sprinkler has been running, however. Why rely on your memory when a timer can shut off the water automatically after a preset time has elapsed or a certain number of gallons of water has been dispensed? For details about such timers, see page 85.

HAND WATERING

All home gardeners need some hand-watering tools, even if they have an underground sprinkler system or a drip system. For example, you may want to apply liquid or water-soluble fertilizer on an extensive planting with a hose-end sprayer, or on a small one with a watering can. And if you want to knock aphids off your rosebushes, you'll need a hose with a nozzle that concentrates water in a strong stream.

WATERING CANS

Made of plastic or of metals such as copper and galvanized steel, watering cans come in shapes from traditional to whimsical and in many sizes. A 2-gallon container is a good choice: it holds enough water to make the hauling worthwhile but is seldom too heavy to lift. Before buying a metal can, pick it up—if it's heavy while empty, imagine its weight when filled with water (a gallon of water alone weighs more than 8 pounds).

Spout length varies, but a spout that extends at least an inch above the top of the body will allow you to fill the can to capacity. Some spouts are open; those with a removable "rose" (a perforated nozzle that disperses water in a gentle shower) are more versatile. You should be able to fill the can without having to tilt it; also be sure your hose nozzle fits into the top so you don't have to remove it when using the hose for filling.

GARDEN HOSES

A hose can simplify or complicate the task of watering your garden. If you buy an inexpensive type that is prone to kinking, you'll spend more time cursing than watering. A durable, kink-resistant type will last much longer and work more efficiently.

HOSE MATERIALS. The type of material a hose is constructed of determines its durability, flexibility, and weight, as well as how readily it kinks. (Whichever type you choose, be sure the hose has brass rather than plastic end fittings, to minimize the possibility of leaks.)

Unreinforced vinyl hoses are inexpensive and lightweight, but they are also the least durable and most prone to kinking. Reinforced vinyl hoses are lightweight, which is important if you have to move the hose around a lot. Rubber hoses, which have dull surfaces, are

TOP: Hose-end nozzles are among the simplest but most useful watering tools.

BOTTOM: The "rose" at the end of this watering can's spout turns a stream of water into a gentle sprinkle.

NOT SO SIMPLE

Some home gardeners take watering tools that are the hallmarks of a simple system and give them a sophisticated twist. They automate their portable sprinklers and soaker hoses by connecting them to the same kind of control valves and multiple-station timers used in underground sprinkler and drip systems.

the heaviest, toughest, and most expensive types. They're also more fire resistant than vinyl hoses; thus, they're recommended wherever wildfires are a threat. Reinforced rubber/vinyl hoses aren't as heavy or expensive as rubber hoses, but they're flexible and durable.

HOSE SIZES. Garden hoses are sold by their inside diameter—most commonly ½, ⅝, and ¾ inch. (The outside diameter varies according to the hose material.) All hose ends have the same size of threads, however, so they can be connected to any outdoor faucet or hose-end nozzle.

Although the inside diameters differ by only a fraction of an inch, the volume of water that each size can carry varies greatly. A ½-inch-diameter hose delivers only about half the water in the same period of time as a ⅝-inch hose, and about a third as much as a ¾-inch one—that is, when water gushes directly from the hose end. When you attach a sprinkler or hose-end nozzle, those differences in output diminish: a ½-inch hose then delivers as much as 75 to 80 percent of the water its ¾-inch counterpart does.

Hoses are also sold according to length—usually 25, 50, 75, and 100 feet. The longer the hose, the heavier it is—and the more friction builds up as water rubs against the inside of the hose walls, resulting in a loss of water pressure. Rather than use a 100-foot hose to irrigate both near and distant plantings, therefore, you're better off with a 25- or 50-footer to which you can attach additional hoses as needed to extend your reach. (Quick couplers make such connections literally a snap; see page 48.)

SPECIALTY HOSES. Some ½-inch-diameter hoses are sold for both indoor and outdoor use. Outdoors, they screw directly onto a hose bibb; indoors, you usually remove the sink faucet's aerator and attach an adapter that comes with the hose. Some models stretch to 30 or 50 feet, recoiling for easy storage. Typi-

Turn the dial of this multiple-pattern hose-end nozzle to distribute water in a gentle shower, strong stream, or mist.

cally, a watering wand or other nozzle is included with the hose. Though handy for, say, using the kitchen sink as a source for watering potted plants on a nearby deck, keep in mind that these hoses deliver water very slowly—thus, watering a lot of plants can be time-consuming.

HOSE ACCESSORIES

Two types of accessories will make your garden hoses easier to work with, help preserve them as well as your plants, and neaten your yard.

STORAGE DEVICES. The various gadgets for storing garden hoses include hose pots, hangers, reels, and carts. A hose pot sits on the ground—you just coil the hose inside. With a wall-mounted

A simple plastic hose guide

or stand-alone hose hanger, you loop the hose around a hook or arm. Wall-hung and portable hose reels have handles that you turn to wrap the hose around the reel. A hose cart also has a reel, but it's part of a wheeled assembly that makes it easier to move a heavy hose around the landscape. With all types of storage devices, you unwrap, uncoil, or crank out as much of the stored hose as you need each time.

HOSE GUIDES. These contraptions keep a hose clear of plants, so that you don't accidentally topple them as you move the hose around. You sink the hose guides into the ground on the periphery of beds or individual plantings, so that the hose catches on them and stays away from plants. The various hose guides sold range from inexpensive plastic models to much costlier metal or clay types that come in decorative shapes.

HOSE ATTACHMENTS

A variety of add-ons is available to attach to your hose. Each performs a valuable function, allowing you to get more utility from a hose.

A hose-end sprayer makes it easy to apply fertilizer over a large area.

HOSE-END NOZZLES. Watering directly from an open-ended hose isn't always satisfying—often you need to diffuse the force of the water or concentrate it into a stronger stream. Once nozzles were restricted to just a few types, but now choices abound in both metal and plastic.

Some emit water in a single pattern; they're activated by turning the water on, by pulling a trigger, or by twisting a section. Twist-type nozzles usually adjust from a fine mist to a hard stream. Other types have multiple patterns—for example, mist, shower, cone spray, soaker, and hard jet; usually, you rotate a dial to the desired pattern and then pull the trigger. (See page 47 for photos of this kind of nozzle in action.)

To extend your reach, attach a long-handled watering wand to your hose. Depending on the model, the nozzle at the end of the wand may have a single pattern or multiple ones.

If your nozzle doesn't incorporate a shutoff valve that allows you to turn off the water from the nozzle instead of at the faucet, you can purchase one separately. Just attach it to the end of the nozzle before connecting the nozzle to the hose.

QUICK COUPLERS. These plastic or brass click-in male/female couplers make mixing and matching attachments a breeze. Thread one onto the end of each outdoor faucet and each hose, hose-end nozzle, and portable sprinkler device. Thereafter, instead of twisting fittings together and risking leaks if the connection isn't tight, you just click the couplers together and pull them apart.

DEEP-ROOT IRRIGATORS. Attach this tool—which resembles a giant hypodermic needle (see the photo on page 104)—to a regular garden hose; then insert it into the ground as you turn the water on. Water travels down a hollow probe and shoots out of holes at the tip. Some types can also supply fertilizer as they water.

Quick couplers let you snap together hose and nozzle.

Shaft length is important only for the comfort of the person using the irrigator, because even the shortest types are long enough to do the job. Don't insert the probe any deeper than 18 inches (less for shallow-rooted plants).

The device is useful for getting water to the root zones of trees growing near sidewalks, patios, or other areas with a minimum of open soil. It also provides a way to get water down through heavy clay soil, and to soak slopes without any runoff. When you're using the irrigator in dense soils, though, don't turn the water on too high or it will back up to the surface.

WATER DIVIDERS

These attachments turn a single faucet into two or more—each branch of the divider has a shutoff valve, so you can use it separately. The most common type is a hose-Y, giving you two branches, but you can also get one that divides the water four ways.

FAUCET EXTENDERS

If an outdoor faucet is seldom used because it's behind shrubbery or requires walking through a flower bed, you can purchase an extender that brings the spigot out by as much as 10 feet. Sometimes billed as a "hose hydrant," the extender provides a short

Both the hose-Y at top and the larger distributor below it have shutoff valves for each outlet. In addition, the four-way divider has a simple mechanical timer controlling all four outlets.

length of garden hose that you attach to your hard-to-reach tap. At the other end of the abbreviated hose is a faucet that attaches to a post, stake, or spike that you push into the ground.

ADDITIONAL FAUCETS

The lack of hose bibbs in certain locations on your exterior house walls may be a nuisance, requiring you to buy extra or longer hoses and drag them farther to get water to plants. Additional, well-placed faucets where needed will provide you with a convenient source of water.

When choosing the exact location, keep in mind that a hose bibb should be high enough to clear a watering can or a bucket. If you're in an area where winter freezes are common, a freezeproof faucet is essential. It has an elongated body that extends well into the basement or crawl space and a valve seat located far back into the body. When you turn off the faucet, the water flow stops back inside the house, protected from cold weather.

The job of hooking a faucet to your household cold-water supply pipe is usually left to a plumber, because of the care that must be taken to avoid drainpipes, electrical conduit, heating ductwork, floor joists, and other obstructions.

PORTABLE SPRINKLERS

The vast assortment of these hose-end devices includes those that will water a space as narrow as a few feet and some that cover a diameter of more than 100 feet. You can buy types that distribute water in circles, part circles, squares, and rectangles. Generally, a sprinkler sprays in a single pattern, though the shape is usually adjustable to some degree. Some models have multiple patterns; you select the one you want by rotating a dial.

Look for a sprinkler whose coverage most closely matches the area to be irrigated—the shape and size of the space that the sprinkler can cover should be listed on the package or in the catalog description. The different types will deliver spray at varying heights, and some are designed to sit on optional tripods so that the spray clears tall plants or other obstacles. (Remember, though, that the higher the spray is thrown, the more subject it is to evaporation and wind drift.)

The many models vary in the amount of water emitted and in the evenness of coverage. Some will work on fairly low pressure, though the "throw," or distance the water travels, will be reduced. You can conduct a catch-can test (see page 95) to determine a sprinkler's output and to locate the driest and wettest spots. Once you know where the gaps in coverage are, you can move the sprinkler around to even things out. As an alternative to moving the sprinkler, you can run more than one at a time, if your water pressure and flow permit it. One option is to operate a couple of well-placed sprinklers, each at the end of its own hose. Or buy sprinklers that can be run in series—they have an extra capped outlet that allows you to connect each sprinkler by garden hose to another sprinkler of the same type.

Whether you run a single sprinkler or more than one, you'll have to pay attention to how well your soil absorbs the sprayed water. If the sprinkler delivers more than the soil can handle, try pulse-irrigating: run the sprinkler until water starts to run off, stop and wait a while, and then run it again as many times as needed until the root zone is wet.

Some sprinklers have a sled base (a platform that sits on the ground); others have a spike base (you stick it into the soil); still others have rollers (you can pull them around the yard). Better-quality sprinklers are made of metal or high-impact plastic.

SLOW-RELEASE WATER

If you can't conveniently get your hose to a plant in an outlying area, try providing it with gelled water that is released slowly. Partly bury the container of gel in the soil, with the gel exposed to the plant's root ball. The number of containers you'll need depends on the plant size. The gel begins to drip water when it comes in contact with soil bacteria, releasing water for as long as a few months.

Gelled water has been used to revegetate sites where piped water is unavailable and for highway plantings. Common uses in home landscapes are to establish newly planted trees in parking strips or far-flung corners of the yard.

ABOVE: Later in the season these plants will be tall enough to block the spray of a sprinkler positioned on the ground. Elevating the sprinkler forestalls the problem.

LEFT: Turn the dial of a multiple-pattern sprinkler to choose the desired spray pattern.

They also tend to have little nozzles or fittings where the water comes out; inexpensive plastic or lightweight aluminum types usually have holes punched into the arms or body of the sprinkler. Some models incorporate a timer that will shut down the sprinkler after a certain amount of water has been delivered or a preset time has elapsed.

SPRINKLER TYPES

The following are the main categories of commonly sold portable sprinklers.

OSCILLATING. These send water sweeping back and forth in a wave. Because water is thrown high, this sprinkler type is best suited to open areas unimpeded by overhanging tree branches. The high arc also means more water lost to evaporation and wind drift. Some of the larger models can water a rectangle or square up to about 3,600 square feet (60 by 60 feet). Better-quality ones have a spray bar that reverses instantly, to prevent overwatering at the far points.

ROTATING. Water whirls out through two or three arms or a spinning baffle in a square, circular, or rectangular pattern, depending on the model. On some, the arms adjust from high to low. This sprinkler type, along with the stationary sprinklers (see below), gives the least uniform coverage, often applying most of the water near the sprinkler.

STATIONARY. This category includes models that resemble salt shakers, rings, and pyramids. Water shoots out through a pattern of holes (square, circular, or rec-

Rotating sprinkler

tangular) in the top of the sprinkler. One model adjusts to spray in six different patterns: a full circle, half circle, small circle, oval, square, and strip. Like rotating sprinklers, these apply water unevenly, typically spraying most of the water close in.

IMPULSE. Just as impact heads in underground sprinkler systems do (see page 57), these sprinklers send out strong pulses of water to wet a circle or any part of it. They're popular because they can cover large areas from one position (as much as 110 feet in diameter), but they can also be adjusted to water smaller areas. Though no portable sprinkler is perfect, this type is considered the most uniform and efficient.

TRAVELING. This device resembling a little tractor is by far the most expensive type of portable sprinkler. It travels along the path of a garden hose that you lay out on

Impulse sprinkler

your lawn, spraying water as it goes. Most models can navigate about 250 feet. A typical traveling sprinkler allows you to set the dial to 15-, 35-, or 50-foot-wide sprays and to light, medium, or heavy soaking. Though this sprinkler type disperses water through rotating arms, its coverage is more even than that of an ordinary rotating sprinkler because it's moving through the area being irrigated.

TOP: Oscillating sprinkler

BOTTOM: Stationary sprinkler

Traveling sprinkler

SOAKER HOSES

A soaker hose emits water along its entire length, and is thus best suited to areas where the soil needs a complete soaking—as in a flower or vegetable bed, along a row of shrubs, or over the root zone of a tree. Don't use it for widely spaced plants.

Though soaker hoses are advertised as attaching easily to an outdoor faucet, one so connected would drip against the wall and all the way to a planting, applying water where it's not wanted.

To overcome this problem, you can simply lay out the hose in the planting, then attach a regular garden hose to it whenever you want to irrigate that area. Another option is to insert a length of regular garden hose as a leader from the spigot and use cut segments of garden hose to interrupt any paths or areas that don't need soaking. The soaker hose and garden hose can easily be connected with metal hose clamps.

TYPES OF SOAKERS

The original soaker hoses were long tubes of canvas, but they've been replaced by an array of more versatile, rot-resistant types, all bearing the name soaker hose. Some—emitter line and laser tubing—are more properly classified as drip system components (see page 72). Of the other products, one is really a sprinkler hose that can be made to soak if laid with the holes facing down; the other oozes water. Both types are commonly available in 25- and 50-foot lengths. Their output depends on water pressure and on flow—the lower the pressure and the less you turn on the faucet, the slower the water will be applied.

SPRINKLER HOSE. This type of hose—some versions of which are plastic, others a combination of plastic and recycled rubber—lies flat when water isn't flowing. When the faucet is turned on, the hose expands, emitting water from uniform holes drilled along one side. When the holes are face up, the water sprays out like a sprinkler. With the holes face down, the water soaks into the soil.

TOP: With its holes facing up, a sprinkler hose sprays water. Flip the hose over, though, and it acts as a soaker.

BOTTOM: Mulching over ooze tubing will help keep hard minerals in the water from clogging its tiny holes.

This type of soaker oozes water.

OOZE TUBING. Sometimes called weeping soaker hose or porous pipe, this product (some brands are made from recycled tires) has thousands of tiny pores. It's available in $1/2$- and $5/8$-inch diameters, with brass hose-thread fittings; you can join two soaker hoses to make a longer one by removing the end cap from one and screwing the hoses together. You can buy these diameters as well as mini ($1/4$-inch-diameter) soaker hose in bulk, without any fittings, for use in drip systems.

Ooze tubing dispenses water most uniformly along its length when it's laid on fairly level terrain, doesn't exceed about 50 feet in length (15 feet for the mini version), and is attached to a pressure regulator that limits the force to 10 pounds per square inch (psi). Turning the faucet on low or placing a washer in the soaker hose connection may lower the pressure sufficiently without a regulator, though you should use one if the hose is watering unevenly or fittings are blowing off.

To discourage clogging, attach a drip-irrigation filter before the pressure regulator. A filter won't screen out hard minerals in your water supply, though—to keep them from contacting air and thereby forming deposits that clog the pores, either bury the hose a few inches deep or cover it with mulch. In any case, you should always flush the soaker hose at least a couple of times a year by removing the end cap to let the water run.

MORE SOPHISTICATED SYSTEMS

The garden hoses and other watering tools discussed on the previous pages are simple, but they apply water imprecisely and take a lot of time to employ. A permanent, automated watering system offers some obvious advantages: it frees you to devote more time to other activities, and it allows you to water while you are away, even for extended periods.

More than that, a well-designed sprinkler or drip system will help you irrigate efficiently. You can give plantings with different moisture requirements just the amount of water they need to thrive. With careful placement of heads, you can avoid watering paths and other areas that don't need it. And you can control the volume of water dispensed, to prevent runoff.

UNDERGROUND SPRINKLERS OR DRIP?

So, assuming that you're tired of hauling hoses and want a permanent irrigation system—which kind should you opt for? Should you install conventional underground sprinklers or drip lines, or should your system consist of both? Your decision will depend on the types of plantings to be irrigated, your terrain, and your water supply's flow and pressure. Of course, your personal preferences—and your budget—are important factors.

Conventional sprinklers are still the best way to water lawns, though underground drip is useful for irrigating odd-shaped patches or narrow strips of turf. Both sprinkler and drip systems are suitable for vegetable gardens, flower beds, and other plantings, though one system may be better than another in specific cases. (See the chapter beginning on page 97 for recommendations on the best ways to water various types of plantings.)

Drip emitters and microsprays apply water much more slowly than conventional sprinklers do. Thus, drip is preferable on hilly terrain, because the water is less likely to run off. If you have a limited amount of water flowing through your pipes—say, 4 or 5 gallons per minute (gpm)—a drip system will enable you to water a lot of plants with that meager amount. With the same flow through conventional sprinklers, you might be able to run only two or three heads at a time—though you can usually cover a larger area with each sprinkler head compared with each individual drip-watering device.

Even if you have adequate flow, you may decide in favor of drip if your water pressure is low. Drip systems work best at pressures under 30 psi, whereas conventional sprinklers need greater force to operate properly.

Underground sprinkler systems tend to be more expensive to install than drip systems, and they take more time to put together. Drip systems, especially simple types screwed onto a hose bibb, require no trenching and are easy to install, even for beginners. They have the added advantage of flexibility—you can easily alter them as your garden grows.

For specifics on underground sprinkler systems, see the section beginning on page 55; for drip systems, refer to the section starting on page 68.

TOP: This underground lawn sprinkler system consists of rotary heads (rotors) that spray in an overlapping pattern.

BOTTOM: Emitter line (drip tubing with preinstalled emitters) waters both young vegetables and an apple tree.

First Steps

Before you start laying out pipelines and choosing irrigation heads, you need to take some preliminary steps. These will speed you along the road to a finished system, regardless of the type.

Gathering Information

Be sure to have on hand the relevant information about your water supply—refer to the chapter beginning on page 33 for instructions on how to determine your water meter size, service line size and type (PVC, copper, or galvanized steel), water pressure, and flow rate. Remember, don't allocate more than 75 percent of your home's flow rate for irrigation—have that reduced figure in mind as you plan your system.

Also check with your local building department about the type of backflow preventer required (see page 39) and whether you need any permits or are subject to any restrictions when installing an irrigation system. If you intend to dig trenches, find out where your sewer, gas, telephone, or other lines are buried by calling the applicable utility companies.

Mapping Your Property

You'll need a scale drawing showing all of the parts of your property to which your irrigation system will extend, including where pipe will be buried and the timer located. Such a map typically includes at least a part of the house and garage, the driveway, walkways, fences, lawn, planting beds, trees and other large individual plants, outdoor faucets, your house water service line, and any additional buried pipes (if you're planning to trench). If you have a septic tank and leach field, you should note their locations and dimensions as well.

Use a 50- or 100-foot tape to measure the relevant areas; note all dimensions on a rough sketch. Then redraw the sketch to scale on graph paper; choose an easy scale, such as one square equaling 1 or 2 feet. You may want to note which planting areas are sunny or shady and mark any slopes, giving the approximate elevation changes in feet. Be sure to mark the location where you intend to tap into the house's water supply.

Establishing Hydrozones

On a copy of your scale drawing, break the planting areas that will be irrigated into hydrozones, groups of plants sharing the same moisture needs (see page 11). Take into account exposure, because plants in hot, sunny spots will need more frequent watering than those in cooler, shadier locations. Also consider soil types: plants growing in a porous container mix, for example, should be watered more often than those in clay soil. Decide on

A Sample Property Map

A Sample Hydrozone Plan

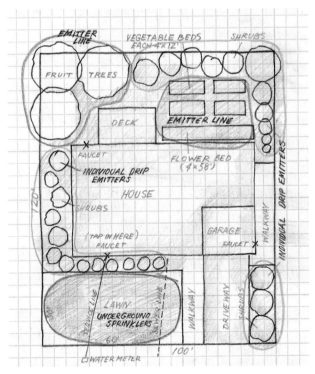

Start by making a scale drawing of your property, noting the various plantings to be irrigated and all relevant dimensions. Mark the intended point of connection—in this sample plan, at the outside faucet closest to the service line.

Group the plantings that share the same moisture needs and decide how to water each group—here, lawn by underground sprinklers, fruit trees by emitter line, vegetable and flower beds by emitter line, and shrubs by individual drip emitters.

CONNECTING TO YOUR HOUSE WATER SUPPLY

A small drip system can be screwed directly onto an outdoor faucet. For multicircuit irrigation systems, you'll have to tap into your water pipes—at a faucet or in the service line, either outdoors or at a basement meter. (See page 39 for information on choosing a location.) When doing so, install a shutoff valve so that you can turn off water to the irrigation system without interrupting flow to the house. From the shutoff valve run pipe to the control valves you'll be putting in for your irrigation system.

Remember to shut off the main water supply first, before the point of connection. If you're apprehensive about tapping into your water pipes, leave this aspect of the job to a professional.

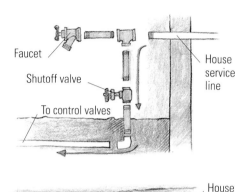

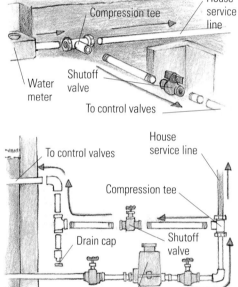

AT AN OUTSIDE FAUCET

With this method, you avoid cutting pipe. Remove the faucet and install a 1/2- or 3/4-inch brass or galvanized tee (a T-shaped fitting); choose one with different-size outlets if you want to connect 3/4-inch irrigation pipe to 1/2-inch faucet pipe. Reattach the faucet; then install a nipple (a short length of pipe threaded at each end) in the stem of the tee and connect a shutoff valve to that.

AT THE SERVICE LINE OUTDOORS

Remove a short section of pipe in the service line, leaving just enough of a gap to slide on a compression tee. Slip the tee over each end of the cut pipe; then tighten the compression nuts. Install a nipple in the stem of the tee and attach a shutoff valve to it. For easy access to the valve, place it in a valve box.

AT A BASEMENT METER

Cut out a short piece of the service line just beyond the water meter. Install a compression tee and a shutoff valve, as described for the outdoor service line connection. Then drill a hole through the basement wall above the foundation for the outgoing pipe, making the hole just large enough to accommodate the pipe. Install a drain cap at the lowest part of the entire assembly, to allow the system to drain before winter.

Note: Not all experts agree that you can use a compression tee in this situation; you may want to ask your irrigation or plumbing supplier about alternatives.

---

the type of watering system you'll employ for each hydrozone—for example, sprinklers or drip emitters.

When you actually plan your sprinkler or drip system, you'll be using this drawing as an aid in plotting the circuits, which are groups of watering devices connected to their own separate control valves. Only plants with the same basic watering requirements should be on the same circuit—hence the reason for initially hydrozoning your diagram. If a hydrozone is small enough, you may be able to include all of the watering devices in it on a single circuit. If your home's water supply is insufficient for all of the devices to work at the same time, you'll have to break the hydrozone into two or more circuits.

CHOOSING A SUPPLIER

If you're new to irrigation systems, you'll probably want to deal with a local supplier rather than a mail-order one, assuming you have a choice. Irrigation stores that supply homeowners are often

very helpful in reviewing plans and advising on installation. You'll appreciate a store that is open on weekends so you can dash over for extra parts. If you're devoting Saturdays to putting in a system, you don't want to be stopped cold for the lack of a part.

You'd be wise to buy all of your materials from the same store, so that all of your components are compatible. There's no need to stick to the same brand, however—one maker may produce excellent sprinklers, whereas another offers superior valves or timers. Some manufacturers make lower-grade components for residential use; consult your supplier to get the same parts that professionals would use.

If you don't know of any irrigation suppliers locally, look in the Yellow Pages under "Irrigation Systems & Equipment" or "Sprinklers—Lawn & Garden."

Seek out a well-stocked local supplier.

UNDERGROUND SPRINKLER SYSTEMS

These permanent systems, with their network of underground pipes linking sprinkler heads that spray on command, are the traditional way to water lawns in regions where rainfall is skimpy or sporadic. Some people use sprinklers throughout the garden, but others prefer more water-conserving drip irrigation beyond the lawn and perhaps the ground covers.

Conventional sprinklers operate at high pressure (you'll have to start out with considerably more than 30 psi, even for the types requiring the least pressure) and high volume (output is measured in gallons per minute, or gpm). Although these devices once had a reputation as water wasters, modern sprinklers apply water much more precisely, thanks largely to improvements in head design. Of course, a sprinkler system's actual efficiency depends on proper layout, operation, and maintenance.

Depending on the size of the area to be irrigated, putting in your own sprinkler system can be time-consuming and tedious—and hiring someone to take it off your hands can be expensive. But with a little careful planning, you can streamline the various tasks, turning installation into a satisfying do-it-yourself project. To lessen the chance of problems, familiarize yourself with the various parts of a sprinkler system before you start designing one.

BASIC COMPONENTS

A conventional underground sprinkler system consists of control valves, pipes and pipe fittings, risers, and sprinkler heads. Incorporate a timer to automate the system.

These remote-control antisiphon valves are grouped in a manifold.

CONTROL VALVES

Each valve controls the flow of water from the main supply line to the sprinklers on a particular circuit. Manual control valves are common in areas where rain does much of the watering in summer. In drier regions, sprinkler systems tend to be automated and thus have remote-control valves—you may see them labeled as solenoid valves. (*Solenoid* refers to the part of the valve that acts as a switch when signaled by the timer.)

Both antisiphon and in-line control valves are sold. A circuit's antisiphon valve—a control valve combined with a backflow preventer—must be located at least 12 inches above the highest sprinkler on that circuit. An in-line valve, installed underground in the pipeline and protected in a valve box, is used when a single backflow preventer is located at the beginning of the system.

Manufacturers list flow and pressure ranges for their valves, so choose a model that will work for you. The most common valve sizes (and the most economically priced) are ¾ and 1 inch. Both plastic and brass versions are available. Brass is sometimes required by local codes—for example, in San Francisco, where earthquake safety is a concern.

PIPES

The main pipe materials used in underground sprinkler systems are two types of plastic: polyvinyl chloride (PVC) and polyethylene.

Both can be used in cold-winter regions, as long as they are buried below the frost line and all the water is drained or blown out of them with compressed air before the ground freezes in winter. Most professionals use PVC for the irrigation main line (the pipes that run from the point of connection to the control valves), even if they use polyethylene for the lateral lines (the pipes that run from each control valve to the sprin-

A part-circle spray head waters a section of lawn.

TAKE IT EASY

If you want to replace your portable sprinkler with something a little more sophisticated but don't want to invest in a traditional underground system, here's an alternative: an easy-to-install kit containing a special type of polyethylene hose, several self-draining pop-up sprinklers, and hose-clamp fittings.

If you live in a freezing climate, this choice will have particular appeal: the polyethylene hose can be buried just beneath the soil surface instead of below the frost line, yet it can be left in place over winter. One caveat is that you must have good flow and pressure to operate the full-circle sprinklers—each one covers about a 20-foot diameter at 40 psi and delivers nearly 3 gpm. Although water delivery is typically less precise and customized than with a standard underground sprinkler system, this type of kit makes a good backup for nature in rainy-summer climates.

The sprinklers have built-in barbed fittings that you insert into the hose; you just tighten the clamps over the connections. Connect the polyethylene hose to an outdoor faucet with a short length of regular garden hose. You can attach your own timer at the faucet to automate the system. Before winter arrives, unhook the connection hose and bring it indoors; cap the end of the polyethylene hose to keep out critters. The rest of the system, including pop-ups, can remain in place.

klers). Some areas require copper for the irrigation main, so check your local codes.

Both types of plastic pipe come in a range of sizes, though ¾ inch, 1 inch, and 1¼ inches are the most widely used for residential sprinkler systems.

PVC. This rigid white pipe is sold in lengths of 10 and 20 feet, with standard and flared ends. The standard end of one pipe fits into the flared end of the next pipe or into a fitting, and a solvent is used to cement the parts together. (See page 64 for instructions on working with this pipe.)

The flared ends of several diameters of PVC pipe

One kind of PVC pipe has the word *class* in its name—Class 120, Class 160, Class 200, and Class 315. The higher the number, the thicker the wall, and the more pressure the pipe can bear (the number actually refers to the psi rating of 1-inch-diameter pipe). An older system bearing the word *schedule*—Schedule 40 and Schedule 80—is based on the dimensions of iron pipe. Many pros specify Schedule 40, which will stand up to constant pressure, for irrigation mains; they use the thinner-walled Class 200 for lateral lines, which carry water only when the circuit is in operation.

Schedule 80 is a gray pipe with more resistance to ultraviolet light than white PVC. It's used above ground—for example, to join elevated antisiphon valves to buried pipe and for stationary sprinkler risers.

POLYETHYLENE. Flexible black pipe sold in large coils, polyethylene is a thicker-walled, larger-diameter version of the tubing long used in drip systems. Its size enables it to operate with higher flow and pressure than drip tubing. Connections to it are made with barbed fittings and hose clamps.

FITTINGS

These plastic pieces for joining sections of pipes include tees (T shaped), elbows (L shaped), couplings (straight), crosses (attachable to pipe at each of four outlets), reducer bushings (larger at one outlet than the other), and caps (to close the end of a line). They provide flexibility by allowing you, for example, to make 90-degree turns, branch a line in several directions, and join pipes of different sizes.

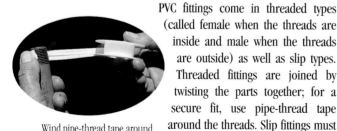

Wind pipe-thread tape around the threads for a tight seal.

PVC fittings come in threaded types (called female when the threads are inside and male when the threads are outside) as well as slip types. Threaded fittings are joined by twisting the parts together; for a secure fit, use pipe-thread tape around the threads. Slip fittings must be cemented with solvent.

The various PVC slip fittings on the left must be cemented to pipe; the threaded fittings on the right screw onto or into other threaded parts.

You may see a PVC tee listed as S × S × S: this means that all three outlets are slip fittings that must be cemented to the pipe. One listed as S × S × T has two side outlets that are slip fittings needing cementing, but a third outlet that is threaded. This is the sort of tee required at a sprinkler location—PVC pipe is glued to the two horizontal outlets, and a threaded riser is screwed into the outlet at the top. (Sometimes the threaded parts of a fitting are described as FIPT, for female iron pipe thread, or MIPT, for male iron pipe thread—a holdover from the days of iron pipe.)

A street elbow, or street ell, is an L-shaped fitting with female threads on one end and male threads on the other. It is commonly used in constructing swing joints (see the section on risers, below).

Fittings for polyethylene pipe are either barbed for insertion into the pipe or threaded for joining with other threaded parts such as risers. A polyethylene tee listed as insert × insert × insert is barbed on all three outlets, for pushing into three sections of pipe. A tee listed as insert × insert × T is suitable for a sprinkler location, like the PVC fitting described above. The two horizontal outlets are inserted into pipe, and a threaded riser is screwed onto the vertical threaded outlet.

RISERS

These are vertical pieces of pipe connecting the underground line either to stationary or to pop-up sprinklers. Options include flexible polyethylene risers that you can buy precut to the desired height, as well as cutoff types that give you a choice of heights. Also available are cutoff riser extensions that you can add below the sprinkler to elevate it. Another product is an adjustable riser (see at right) that allows you to raise or lower the sprinkler as needed.

Adding a new piece to the riser puzzle is the swing joint, a type of flexible connection between the pipe and the

As your plants grow, slide the adjustable riser up so that the spray clears the foliage.

sprinkler. The swing joint moves up and down, making height adjustments easy. For example, you can substitute a sprinkler of a different height for the one you had previously and still position it properly. You can build your own swing joint from three street elbows and a nipple (a short length of threaded pipe); all of these parts are available through irrigation and plumbing suppliers. Or you can buy a ready-made swing joint (see at right).

Specialty products sold under various brand names and consisting of thick-walled polyethylene tubing serve the same purpose as a traditional swing joint. You can also use them like an extension cord—for example, locating pipe just outside a bed but using the tubing to stretch the sprinklers all the way to the bed's inside edge.

SPRINKLERS

In addition to being less wasteful than they were in the past, today's sprinklers offer many more features. A good understanding of the different types of sprinklers will enable you to choose the ones that will work best in your situation.

SPRINKLER TYPES. There are two basic categories of sprinklers: spray heads and rotary heads (rotors). Spray heads emit a fixed spray, whereas rotors—both gear-driven and impact types—have heads that move as they shoot out streams of water. In the gear-driven rotor, water turns a series of gears in the sprinkler body, causing the head to rotate. In the impact rotor, water hits a spring-loaded arm, causing the head to turn. Because of the constant slapping of water against the arm of an impact model, durable brass is often chosen instead of plastic. If you plan to run your sprinklers early in the morning and you are sensitive to noise, choose the quieter gear-driven rotors.

Spray heads are suited to small areas, throwing water in up to about a 15-foot radius. They operate best at 30 psi—at lower pressures their coverage may be compromised, and at much higher ones they tend to mist or fog. With higher-than-recommended pressure, you may have to install a pressure reducer or use spray heads with a flow control adjustment.

A ready-made swing joint connects the sprinkler to a PVC pipe fitting. Move the swing joint up or down to position the sprinkler at just the right level.

A spray-head sprinkler dispenses water in a fanlike spray, the pattern of which is determined by its nozzle.

Rotors suitable for home landscapes cover more territory than do spray heads, up to about a 45-foot radius. They typically need more force, though (about 40 to 50 psi), to cover those distances and to reverse the arc at the end of each rotation. At low pressure, rotors tend to apply most of the water at the end of their arc. If you have low pressure but want to run rotors, you may have to install a booster pump.

Spray heads put out more water in the smaller area they cover and so have a

The gears within this rotor sprinkler cause its head to rotate quietly.

higher precipitation rate (the amount of water, in inches, applied per hour) than rotors do. Because the rotating sprinklers apply water more slowly, they have to run longer. However, rotors are economical in large areas: you'll need fewer heads, which means fewer circuits, fewer valves, and a timer with fewer stations.

You can get low-angle and flat-spray heads, both of which are useful for watering slopes (place the heads at the top of the slope) or where low tree branches or wind can deflect spray.

Both spray heads and rotors are available in stationary sprinklers and pop-ups. Spray heads and gear-driven rotors come in pop-ups as tall as 12 inches, but impact pop-ups are generally only a couple of inches high. Modern pop-ups have improved wiper seals, which act like gaskets to prevent water from leaking out around the sprinkler shafts when they pop up.

HOW TO WATER THOSE FEW ODD PLANTS

What if you have some thirsty shrubs on the periphery of a lawn but don't want to set up a separate irrigation circuit for just a few plants? Ordinarily you wouldn't mix head types on a circuit, but here's a trick that works: add a multioutlet emitter to the line. Though actually a drip-irrigation component, this type of emitter can also work at high pressure. Choose one that puts out a lot of water, so that the shrubs will get enough during the relatively brief time run time you've scheduled for lawn irrigation.

Impact sprinklers are so named because the water forcibly strikes an arm, causing the head to turn.

All sprinklers have undergone improvements in recent years to upgrade their performance and durability. For example, spray heads and many gear-driven rotors now have internal filters that keep them from clogging. (Because of their larger openings, impact and gear-driven rotors with high-output nozzles are naturally clog resistant, making them popular in rural areas where "dirty" water is often a problem.) And both spray heads and rotors are now available with built-in check valves that prevent water from seeping out of the sprinklers when the system is turned off, flooding low areas.

Some manufacturers build pressure-compensating devices (PCDs) into certain spray-head models or offer them as an optional part (you may have to go to an irrigation specialty store to find them). They help regulate water pressure, so that the first sprinkler on the line won't use all of the pressure and prevent succeeding heads from working properly. They also prevent fogging and drift if water pressure is high. By changing the size of a PCD, you can also reduce the "throw" of the sprinkler (to prevent overspray), which is more effective than throttling down on the screw on top of the sprinkler.

Color-coded PCDs fit underneath nozzles to help regulate water pressure and prevent overspray.

NOZZLES. With both stationary and pop-up spray heads, the sprinkler body and nozzle are often sold separately. The nozzle determines the sprinkler's pattern, as well as the radius of throw and gallonage (each nozzle has a range for these, but the exact figures will depend on your water pressure).

Most manufacturers provide a good selection of set-pattern nozzles: 90° (quarter circle), 120° (third circle), 180° (half circle), 240° (two-thirds circle), 270° (three-quarters circle), and 360° (full circle). For odd shapes, variable-arc nozzles (VANs) are invaluable—you can adjust the nozzle to the portion of a circle desired, usually from 0° to about 330°.

Spray-head manufacturers are now also offering a broader selection of nozzles for small areas. Many companies offer sprinklers with a 5-, 8-, or 10-foot radius, which is more precise for

These spray-head nozzles determine the spray pattern, the amount of water applied, and the throw distance.

This strip-pattern nozzle will water a rectangle.

small planting areas than the typical 12- or 15-foot radius most commonly sold. Strip nozzles that water in squares and rectangles also come in more sizes than before, allowing you to cover strips as narrow as 2 feet.

Most spray heads on the market today have matched-precipitation-rate nozzles, meaning that water is emitted by the various patterns proportionately—a quarter-circle nozzle puts out a quarter of the water of its companion full-circle nozzle, rather than delivering the same amount over less area, as was the case with old sprinklers. You can mix heads with different arcs and radius throws on the same circuit but still get uniform water distribution. Newer types of nozzles also seal themselves when the irrigation system is off, protecting them from debris.

All rotors have adjustable arcs (how you make the adjustment depends on the sprinkler head model and manufacturer). The arc ranges vary—on some heads, for example, the arc may adjust from 20° to 340°, on others from 45° to 315°. With gear-driven rotors, you generally get the body and a rack or set of interchangeable, color-coded nozzles. To equalize the water going to each area—say, when running two heads with different arcs side by side—you'd use a larger- or smaller-size nozzle on the second to get more or less output from it.

Impact rotors usually have a built-in nozzle that can be changed to a larger or smaller size, though not as easily as you change the gear-driven models. To address the problem of more water falling in a smaller arc than in a larger one, the pros typically put the different arc sizes on separate circuits and run them for different lengths of time. For example, they would operate heads set to a half circle for twice as long as those set to a quarter circle, to equalize the amount of water dispensed.

A simple twist changes the spray pattern of a variable-arc nozzle to the desired segment of a circle.

TIMERS

A timer, or controller, linked to your remote-control valves by underground wire will allow you to schedule waterings for all of your circuits. For information on the various kinds of timers available, see the section beginning on page 85.

The nozzles of these sprinklers throw just short of the tree trunk.

PLANNING YOUR SYSTEM

Designing your sprinkler system on paper will help you think matters through; your final plan will guide you when ordering materials and serve as a permanent record of where the pipes are buried and where the valves and other elements are located.

You can plan your own system or ask your irrigation supplier or other professional for help. Many sprinkler manufacturers provide detailed worksheets and installation directions; some will even plan a system specifying their products if you send them a scale drawing of the area to be irrigated.

When handling the design yourself, you may want to consult sprinkler catalogs from the major manufacturers (see if any are available locally at an irrigation supply outlet or check the resource list on page 111). Or you can just lay out the components as explained in the next section and then shop for parts that fit your design. At that point, your supplier may suggest improvements or tweak the design.

LOCATING THE SPRINKLERS

Laying out this key element of your system is a lot easier than it used to be, thanks to more choices in sprinkler throw distances and patterns. Also helpful are variable-arc nozzles, which have simplified the task of getting water to odd-shaped areas.

First, make a copy of the scale drawing of your property divided into hydrozones (see page 53). The best course is to tackle each hydrozone separately. The largest one, and perhaps the only one requiring conventional sprinklers, may be the lawn; other hydrozones may be candidates for drip.

HEAD-TO-HEAD SPRINKLER COVERAGE

For uniform coverage, the spray from one sprinkler head should reach the adjoining head.

REMEMBER THESE RULES. As you mark sprinkler locations, keep the following guidelines in mind.

Use as few sprinklers as possible to achieve good coverage. If you have a 30-foot-wide lawn, as in the sample plan, you're better off using rotors that throw that distance rather than twice as many spray heads that distribute water only half as far. Remember, the more sprinklers you use the more circuits, valves, and timer stations you'll need, the more trenches you'll have to dig, and the more pipe you'll have to lay. That all adds up to a more complicated, more expensive system.

So, to keep the number of sprinklers to a minimum, you'll have to choose those that throw as far as possible without overspraying the area. As you read in the section on sprinklers (see page 57), spray heads dispense water in up to about a 15-foot radius, rotors in up to about a 45-foot radius. If you have a large lawn but lack adequate pressure for rotors, you may want to compare the cost of installing a booster pump with that of significantly increasing the number of sprinkler heads and valves.

Always overlap sprinkler sprays. This means that the spray from one sprinkler should extend all the way to the adjoining sprinkler, a principle that the pros call head-to-head coverage. To make this work, you'll need an equal amount of space between sprinklers. The various sprinkler types usually have some weak spots in their spray pattern (except for impacts, most sprinklers throw more water at the outer edge of the pattern than near the head), so overlapping will ensure more uniform coverage.

DRAWING IN THE SPRINKLERS. On the copy of your scale drawing, start by planning coverage for any square and rectangular spaces, because free-form areas and curves will take a little more time. In the regular-shaped areas, mark sprinkler locations in the corners and along the perimeter.

The proportions of some areas make the job of placement easy. With an area that divides evenly, like the 30- by 60-foot lawn in the sample plan, the solution quickly becomes clear—in this case, six 30-foot rotors (one in each corner and one in the middle of each 60-foot side).

For spaces that aren't mathematically proportionate, start with a sprinkler in each corner and then figure the fewest number of sprinklers that each side will accommodate (keeping in mind the maximum throws for spray heads and rotors, and also allowing for head-to-head coverage). Depending on the area, you may have to place sprinklers in the middle as well.

Using a pencil compass, draw the arc needed for each head: quarter-circle sprinklers in the corners, half-circle ones along the edges, and full-circle ones in the middle. On narrow bits of lawn, you can use strip spray heads, which throw water in squares and rectangles—or, if there's room, a series of half-circle spray heads on each side.

For large curving or irregular areas, you'll be able to adjust the arc on rotors to fit the area. For smaller ones, rely on variable-arc nozzles (the series of photos on page 58 shows how the

DRAWING IN THE SPRINKLERS

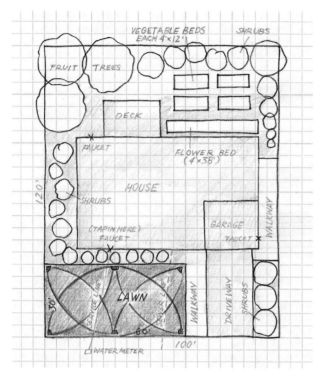

Mark sprinkler locations on the lawn, attempting to use the fewest sprinklers possible. It's clear that rotors will achieve that goal better than spray heads will (see the worksheet samples below). Use a pencil compass to draw in the overlapping sprays.

spray pattern can be changed). If you can't avoid some overspray with these or other sprinklers, try to keep the excess to a minimum and make sure it isn't directed at the side of your house, a fence, or another structure.

Repeat this procedure for each hydrozone. Note whether any hydrozone should have low-trajectory heads, so that the spray will be less subject to wind drift.

PLOTTING CIRCUITS

A circuit is a group of sprinklers controlled by the same valve. There are two reasons for breaking your system into circuits. First, few homes' water supplies have high enough flow or pressure to run a lot of sprinklers at once. Second, by having separate circuits for plantings with different moisture needs, you can give each the appropriate amount of water.

In plotting circuits, group only the same type of sprinklers—for example, impact heads must go on a different circuit than spray heads. You can put pop-ups on the same circuit as stationary heads, as long as all of the sprinklers are fitted with the same kind of nozzle.

Also remember that the total gallonage of all the sprinklers on a single circuit should not exceed 75 percent of your flow rate. If your water flows at the rate of 12 gpm, for example, no single circuit should exceed 9 gpm. To determine a proposed circuit's total gallonage, you'll need to know the output of each sprinkler. You can get this information from a sprinkler catalog, a manufacturer's workbook, or an irrigation supplier—or consult the chart on the facing page for some common throw distances and output rates.

ROTORS OR SPRAY HEADS?

Here's how to decide whether rotors or spray heads are a better choice for watering a given area—for example, the 30- by 60-foot lawn in the sample plan. First, let's assume that your flow rate is 12 gpm. That means you can simultaneously run sprinklers whose outputs add up to no more than 9 gpm (because only 75 percent of your total flow rate can be allocated to irrigation).

To cover the lawn, you would therefore need six 30-foot rotors or fifteen 15-foot spray heads. Using the chart on the facing page as a guide, mark in sprinkler gallonage rates on each of your tentative plans. Because the total rotor outputs don't exceed 9 gpm, they would fit on a single circuit. The spray-head outputs far exceed the allowable amount, however, so those heads would have to be divided into four circuits.

In this case, rotors are more economical and require less installation work—but note that you'll have to run them longer than spray heads, because they apply water more slowly.

ROTORS

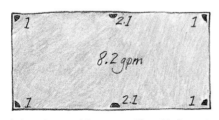

4 quarter circles × 1 gpm = 4.0 gpm	Allowable flow = 9 gpm
2 half circles × 2.1 gpm = 4.2 gpm	(75% of 12-gpm flow rate)
————	Rotors fit on one circuit.
8.2 gpm	

SPRAY HEADS

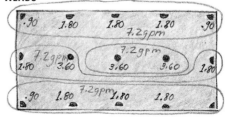

4 quarter circles × .90 = 3.6 gpm	Allowable flow = 9 gpm
8 half circles × 1.80 = 14.4 gpm	(75% of 12-gpm flow rate)
3 full circles × 3.60 = 10.8 gpm	Spray heads need four circuits.
————	(28.8 ÷ 9 gpm = 3.2)
28.8 gpm	

SOME SPRINKLER OUTPUT RATES

Here are the output rates of some commonly specified sprinklers, listed in gpm. The many models differ, so check with your supplier before making a final plan.

SPRAY HEADS (OPERATING AT 30 PSI)

RADIUS OF THROW	ARC PATTERNS					
	360° ●	270° ◗	240° ◗	180° ◗	120° ◢	90° ◣
8 ft.	1.00 gpm	.75 gpm	.70 gpm	.50 gpm	.35 gpm	.25 gpm
10 ft.	1.60 gpm	1.20 gpm	1.00 gpm	.80 gpm	.50 gpm	.40 gpm
12 ft.	2.40 gpm	1.80 gpm	1.60 gpm	1.20 gpm	.80 gpm	.60 gpm
15 ft.	3.60 gpm	2.70 gpm	2.40 gpm	1.80 gpm	1.20 gpm	.90 gpm

STRIP PATTERNS

4 × 30 ft.	1.10 gpm
9 × 18 ft.	1.35 gpm

ROTORS (OPERATING AT 40 TO 50 PSI)*

RADIUS OF THROW	
30 ft.	1.00 gpm
35 ft.	1.80 gpm
40 ft.	2.70 gpm
45 ft.	5.20 gpm

* For proper coverage, typically you must set some rotors to different arcs than others—in the sample plan on the facing page, some of the rotors will spray in quarter circles and others in half circles. Using the same nozzle for all the heads is inadvisable, because twice as much water will fall in areas covered by the smaller arcs than in those covered by larger ones. You can solve this problem with a careful choice of nozzles. For example, if you use a 1-gpm nozzle for your quarter circles, pick a nozzle using approximately twice as much water for your half circles; then tighten down the diffusing screw to get the proper radius. In effect you are creating matched precipitation rates, just as the manufacturers do for you with spray heads.

Write the output in gpm of each sprinkler next to its location on your plan. Then circle groups of sprinklers serving plants with similar water needs. Assign as many sprinklers to a circuit as you can without exceeding your flow allotment. If a circuit outstrips your flow, split it into two or allocate some of the sprinklers to a circuit that still has some available flow.

LOCATING THE CONTROL VALVES AND TIMER

You could place each control valve at the beginning of the circuit it operates, but clustering the valves in a manifold (a grouping of valves) facilitates wiring them to the timer.

Choose a spot where you won't be sprayed if you have to reach a valve while the system is operating. You may decide on one manifold for the front yard and another for

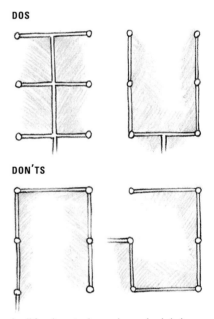

ROUTING DOS AND DON'TS

DOS

DON'TS

In all four layouts shown above, pipe is being routed to six sprinklers (represented by the circles). The H- and U-shaped routes at the top are efficient, because they equalize the flow of water to each sprinkler. In the poorly laid out routes below them, water travels in an undivided path, making two or three turns. Both flow and pressure would significantly diminish by the time the water reached the last sprinkler.

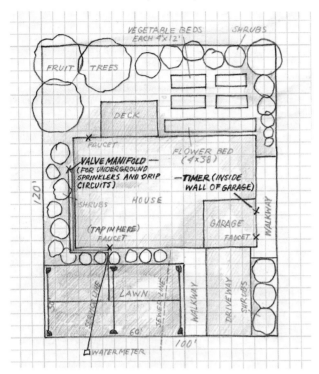

Choose convenient, out-of-view locations for the valve manifold and the timer. When routing the pipe from the manifold to the sprinklers, take a direct path that will distribute water as equally as possible to the six sprinklers. Note that the trench from the point of connection to the valve can carry both lateral and irrigation main pipes.

SIZING PIPE AND VALVES

The pros often use several pipe sizes, because they've calculated the smallest-diameter pipe that will suffice for each part of the system. There's no need for you to do likewise, because you're putting in only one system and pipe is relatively inexpensive. You'll make your job easier by sticking to either one pipe size for the whole system or one for the irrigation main plus a second, smaller size for the laterals.

Properly sized pipe will minimize friction and thus pressure loss, as well as allow water to travel at a safe speed; refer to the chart on page 37 to find an appropriate size. You can always choose a larger-diameter pipe than the one indicated for your flow level, to compensate for low water pressure or long pipe runs.

If the pipe is sized correctly, the valve size isn't important—pressure loss through a valve is minimal compared to pressure loss in pipe runs. Thus, you can use economical ¾- or 1-inch valves, even if the pipe diameter is larger.

the back. Manifolds of elevated valves are often hidden behind shrubbery; if your control valves are in-line types, you can bury the entire assembly underground, in a valve box for easy access.

Locate the timer in a protected spot near an electrical outlet. (See page 87 for more information.)

ROUTING THE PIPE

You'll be laying out pipelines for the irrigation main as well as for all the lateral lines containing the sprinklers. To minimize pressure loss, avoid unnecessarily long runs or lines with many turns. Also try to avoid routing pipe through areas with many tree roots or under driveways and other pavement. On a slope, lay as much pipe as possible horizontally, along the contours of the land, rather than up and down.

On your scale drawing, sketch in the irrigation main. If the valves are located in a single manifold, you'll need just one pipeline; for an additional manifold, continue the pipe from the first manifold to the second. If each valve is located separately near the circuit it controls, sketch a pipeline to the nearest valve and run pipe from that valve to each subsequent valve.

To route the pipe for each circuit, start at the valve and work out toward the sprinklers. A good way to equalize the water supply to the sprinklers is to branch the pipe so that roughly half of the water is directed to half of the sprinklers. The pros divide the flow as soon as possible, usually creating H and U shapes (see the illustrations on page 61).

When leading away from a valve manifold to a circuit, you may be able to lay two or even three pipes in a single trench. Look for such opportunities to save trenching work.

ASSEMBLING A SHOPPING LIST

Checking your scale drawing, count the number of control valves, the number and types of fittings and sprinkler heads, and the total length of each pipe size (for every 20 feet of pipe add 1 foot, to account for fitting overlap and sag in the trench). To figure out how much low-voltage wire to buy for connecting the valves and timer, see page 87.

The tools you'll need for installation are shown in the photo at right. Either a PVC cutter or a hacksaw will cut pipe, but the former is more efficient. Primer and solvent are also necessary, for joining PVC pipes and fittings.

Installation tools include, clockwise from left, a trench shovel, hacksaw, pipe wrench, pick, tape measure, string, mallet, stakes, utility knife, screwdriver, and PVC cutter.

INSTALLING YOUR SYSTEM

Once you have all the necessary materials on hand, you can start putting in your sprinkler system. There's no need to install the whole system at once, especially if the yard is already landscaped and you have only the odd weekend to work on the project.

Of the various installation tasks described below, trenching is listed first. However, don't start digging until you're certain of where you'll tie into your water pipes (see page 54 for instructions on making the connection) and where you'll locate your valve manifold. Also, review your sketch to be sure you've chosen the most economical route, requiring the least amount of trenching.

You can construct your manifold ahead of time and then connect it to your pipeline when you're ready. You'll find it easier to install your system if you start from the water source and proceed out toward the sprinklers.

DIGGING TRENCHES

This aspect of installation can be hard work, so you may prefer to rent a trenching machine or hire someone else to do the digging for you.

A trenching machine makes quick work of digging underground channels for irrigation pipe in lawns and unplanted beds.

When trenching yourself, soften up hard ground by watering it with a portable sprinkler a couple of days before you begin. Consulting your master plan, lay out each trench with string and stakes so you'll know exactly where to excavate. Study your plan to make sure you haven't missed an opportunity to assign more than one pipe to a trench instead of digging separate trenches. Be careful to avoid utility lines, especially if you are using a trenching machine.

In mild-winter climates, trenches 8 to 12 inches deep are adequate, though you may want to dig deeper to avoid hitting irrigation pipes later on, when you're working in the garden. A trench depth of 18 inches is sufficient in most areas where hard freezes occur. In very cold climates, consult your local irrigation supplier or Cooperative Extension agent for the appropriate depth.

For hand digging, equip yourself with a sturdy trench shovel and a pick. If sprinklers are to be positioned on a bed's inside perimeter, avoid trenching right in the

PULLING PIPE

Rather than dig actual trenches, contractors in northern climates often install polyethylene pipe with a tractor and vibratory plow, also called a pipe puller. The machine pulls the pipe underground to a specific depth, creating very little damage even in an established lawn. There are no trenches to fill after the pipe is in place.

The contractors start out by marking each sprinkler location; then they hook the pipe to the plow and pull all of the pipe runs into place.

DIGGING UNDER WALKWAYS

The best way to excavate under paved areas is to tear away the soil with a strong blast of water. You can attach a garden hose to a length of threaded galvanized steel pipe that is larger than your irrigation pipe and that will act as a sleeve for it. Turn on the water full force; remove the hose once the soil is wet enough and drive the pipe through with a sledgehammer. Before feeding your irrigation pipe through, cover its end with duct tape to keep debris out.

As an alternative, you can buy a kit containing a power nozzle and a couple of fittings that will allow you to drive PVC pipe through the soil. Use the fittings to attach the power nozzle to the front of the pipe and your garden hose to the rear. Turn on the faucet and work the pipe through (turn off the water every once in a while to let the water soak in).

Tunneling under a driveway is not an easy task. If you must cross a driveway, consider having a contractor excavate, install large conduit, and repave. On new properties, laying the appropriate pipes under walkways and driveways will save you time and trouble later on when you install your irrigation system.

bed—it's better to dig parallel but a little distance from the bed, and then use thick-walled polyethylene tubing to move the sprinkler into position (see the section on risers on page 56). When digging in lawn, lay the sod on one side of the trench and the excavated soil on the other; you'll have an easier time restoring the turf later on.

If you decide to use a trenching machine, check with an equipment rental outlet—machines are usually rented by the hour, day, or week. Be sure to get instructions on how to operate the machine before you leave with it. A trencher is ideal for lawns and unplanted areas away from buildings and steep slopes, but don't use one to dig in ground covers or flower beds.

LAYING PIPE

The pipe should be laid as level as possible at the bottom of the trench, though a little unevenness won't be a problem. As you work, try to keep the inside of the pipes as dirt free as possible. (You may be laying low-voltage wire in some pipe trenches leading from the valves toward the timer; see page 87.)

PVC PIPE. When carrying lengths of PVC pipe, be sure not to knock them together or drop them. The pipe can break—or worse, develop a hairline crack that you don't notice until it bursts under normal water pressure when the system is running.

Undoubtedly, you'll have to cut and fit together some sections of pipe. Before cutting, be sure you've allowed for the distance the pipe will extend into the flared end of the adjoining pipe or into a fitting. A PVC pipe cutter makes a cleaner cut than a hacksaw (if you use a saw, scrape off any burrs with a utility knife).

You can lay out all the pipe lengths and fittings first and then go back to make the connections; or you can connect as you go. Join PVC parts together as shown at right (the same principles will apply when you join fittings to pipe). Work rapidly: the plastic solvent adheres quickly, and joints once cemented cannot be broken apart. The drying time is affected by temperature, humidity, and the type of solvent used. Though installers are often advised to wait at least 6 hours before running water through the pipes, check the solvent manufacturer's recommendations on the product label.

POLYETHYLENE PIPE. Unroll the pipe and lay it in the trench, making connections with barbed insert fittings and stainless steel hose clamps. Place a clamp over the pipe, insert a barbed fitting into the end of the pipe, and slide the clamp down, tightening it around the pipe and fittings with a screwdriver.

A PVC cutter severs pipe cleanly, without leaving burrs to be filed smooth.

DRAIN VALVES

Water freezing inside irrigation pipes can cause the pipes to burst. Therefore, in regions where the ground freezes in winter, install an automatic drain valve at the lowest point in each circuit. Many homeowners also have their irrigation systems blown out with compressed air.

Here's how to join sections of PVC pipe. Prop the pipes up out of the trench to make them easier to work with; be sure their ends are clean. You'll get a better joint if you first dissolve the waxy coating on the pipe by applying a primer on the outside of the standard, or cut, end and on the inside of the flared end. Working quickly, brush solvent cement (ask your supplier for a product recommendation) evenly over the primer coat. Twist the pipes together a quarter turn and hold them for about 20 seconds. Wipe off any excess cement.

Each of the in-line remote-control valves in this manifold (protected by a valve box) controls a separate sprinkler circuit. Tee fittings connect the valve inlets to the irrigation main line, and lateral-line pipe leads from each valve outlet to the sprinklers on a particular circuit.

The tops of pop-up lawn sprinklers should be at grade level (lay a board across the trench to find this level)—to protect them from mowers and also to keep them from tripping people. Measure carefully so that you are sure to install a riser of the correct height.

ASSEMBLING THE MANIFOLD

You can assemble your grouping of control valves on a workbench or other convenient place and then take it out to the manifold site when you're ready to hook the valves to the pipe. You'll be attaching some threaded fittings to the valves—wrap pipe-thread tape around the threads and hand-tighten rather than use a wrench and risk stripping the threads inside the valve. Also note that an arrow on the valve indicates the direction of flow (the arrow points toward the outlet leading to the sprinklers).

For an in-line valve manifold (see the left-hand photo above), screw a tee fitting into each valve's inlet. For elevated anti-siphon valves, insert a gray Schedule 80 nipple (it won't degrade in sunlight as much as regular white PVC) of the required length into the valve inlet; screw on a tee at the bottom of the nipple. Spacing the in-line or antisiphon valves at least 6 inches apart for easy access, connect the tees with pipe. For both types of valves, add a stubout (a short length of pipe that you cap off) to accommodate future circuits.

To each in-line valve's outlet, screw in a thread-by-slip adapter. To each antisiphon valve's outlet, screw in another Schedule 80 nipple, attaching a thread-by-slip elbow at the bottom. Position either type of manifold in the desired location and attach the pipe from the irrigation main as well as the pipe leading to the sprinklers.

INSTALLING RISERS

With a tape measure, determine the desired height of each sprinkler head. The top of a pop-up sprinkler should be level with the soil surface, and the riser for a stationary sprinkler should be high enough so that foliage won't block the spray. If you use a cutoff riser, cut it at the desired level. A swing joint (see the riser section on page 56) will make it easy to position the sprinkler.

Cut the pipe at each sprinkler location. Install a tee fitting and attach the riser, making sure that it's perpendicular to the surrounding terrain. This will ensure proper coverage when the sprinkler is running.

After attaching the risers, clear dirt and debris by flushing the system.

FLUSHING THE SYSTEM

Don't wait until you've installed your sprinkler heads to flush the system, because dirt and other debris inside the pipes can rapidly clog the heads.

To flush your system, turn on the water one circuit at a time. You'll be able to see the water gush out of the risers; wait until it runs clear before shutting it off and installing sprinklers.

ATTACHING THE SPRINKLERS

Screw the sprinkler heads to the risers, starting from the valve end and working outward. Because the last few sprinklers on each circuit of a newly installed system are subject to clogging, leave those heads off. Then flush the system once more to get rid of any lingering debris. Once you've finished, attach the remaining sprinklers.

Take care to align the sprinklers so that they spray properly. If the spray direction isn't clearly marked on the heads, check the manufacturer's instructions or consult your irrigation equipment supplier.

INSTALLING THE TIMER

Now's the time to put in a timer, or controller, and connect it to your remote-control valves. For details on these aspects of installation, refer to the section starting on page 85.

TESTING THE SYSTEM

Before filling in the trenches, test the system—but first turn off any water running in the house so that you don't have a dishwasher or washing machine competing with your irrigation system.

After you've switched on the water to the irrigation system at the shutoff valve, turn on each circuit manually at the timer. If none of them comes on, examine the control valves to be sure they're installed in the correct direction: water should flow in the direction of the arrow, toward the sprinklers. If they're properly positioned, the problem is probably electrical—check your wiring at the valves and the timer. If only one circuit balks, inspect the control valve to make sure the flow control isn't turned down. Also check the wiring for that circuit.

If a pop-up sprinkler doesn't pop up, review your plans to verify that the sprinkler really is on the circuit you're testing. If it is, look for debris under the sprinkler. A head (pop-up or stationary) that doesn't spray may mean that the nozzle is clogged (clean it) or that the adjusting screw is turned down too far (loosen it). If a head puts out a weak spray, check the flow control on the valve. If weak spray is evident on several heads near each other, you may have too many sprinklers on the circuit; recheck your plan to see if that circuit's sprinklers exceed the allowable flow.

Make sure that sprinkler spray is aimed at the intended planting, as this part-circle spray head watering a mixed border is.

As you test the system, you may have to adjust a sprinkler's direction, throw, or spray pattern. Direction is often easily altered by turning the sprinkler body or tweaking the riser. Make sure that the spray patterns overlap. Most sprinkler nozzles have an adjusting screw to control the distance the spray is thrown—it's best not to alter the throw by more than about 20 percent. Adjusting the spray pattern on a variable-arc nozzle is easy. With a set-pattern nozzle, you may find that exchanging it for one of a different pattern will give you better coverage. Follow the manufacturer's directions for adjusting the arc of a rotor.

BACKFILLING TRENCHES

As you replace the excavated soil, be sure there are no rocks right around the pipes. Fill each trench to just a little lower than the original soil or sod line; then flood it with water to settle the soil. Add more soil, mounding it slightly, and sprinkle the mound with your hose or portable sprinkler to settle it further. In a lawn, replace the sod that you removed and laid aside.

MAINTAINING YOUR SYSTEM

It's possible to damage pipes with an errant thrust of a shovel while gardening (to fix a break, see the photos at left), but most of your maintenance efforts will be directed toward sprinklers. Normal operation can cause sprinklers to clog, jam, leak, or spray improperly—and, of course, they can be damaged by lawn mowers, cars, and the like. Because faulty sprinklers can waste water as well as harm plants by depriving them of adequate moisture, it's important to conduct monthly or even more frequent inspections during the watering season.

This cracked underground pipe (top) was repaired by cutting out the broken section and cementing an adjustable splice unit to one end and a slip coupling to the other. The two parts were then joined (bottom).

UNCLOGGING SPRINKLER HEADS

A clogged sprinkler will usually force water out at an odd angle, or the spray may be greatly reduced. Brass spray heads clog frequently, because they lack filters. However, any head can become clogged if soil, mineral deposits, insects, and other debris collect in the slits or holes from which the water emerges.

Several times during the season, check the heads for uneven spray patterns while the system is on. Clean the slits or holes with a knife or a piece of thin, stiff wire. If that doesn't work, remove the entire head and clear it of debris.

REPLACING BROKEN SPRINKLERS AND RISERS

To replace a broken head, you'll need to unscrew it by hand or with a wrench and replace it with another of the same kind. Because dirt may have entered the damaged head and traveled downstream, remove all nozzles beyond the break and clean them.

A broken riser may be difficult to extract; it helps to use a stub wrench for additional leverage. If solvent cement was used to install the riser, cut the riser pipe off cleanly and attach a new one, using an adaptor fitting.

As you work, be careful that no soil spills into the line. If soil does get in, you'll have to remove all of the sprinkler heads on the circuit and flush the system until the water runs clear.

ADJUSTING SPRINKLERS

Because water pressure varies during the day, it's important to inspect your system at the time when it's normally in use, even if you have to get up early to do it. Turn each circuit on in sequence and look at the sprinkler heads.

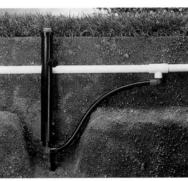

First, note whether the spray from any head is blocked. If that's the case with any lawn sprinklers, keep the grass clipped low around the heads and dethatch—a lawn can gain several inches of height over time from built-up thatch. Often, sprinklers in new shrub and ground cover plantings are installed too low to spray over the mature plants. Solve that problem by replacing the riser with a longer one or by adding a riser extension.

Scrutinize any part-circle sprinklers, especially those along the perimeter of the lawn and planting beds. If any one is spraying off center, gently turn the head or nozzle, or adjust the rotor's arc—following the manufacturer's directions—until it covers the desired area.

Inspect all of the sprinklers for the correct throw and pattern; refer to "Testing the System," on the facing page, for adjustment tips.

You can relocate a sprinkler along the line—perhaps because you've cut into the lawn area to increase the size of an adjacent flower bed—with the help of thick-walled polyethylene tubing used like an extension cord. To substitute a taller pop-up, as shown here, just join the sprinkler—in its new lower position—to the tee in the water pipe; a special stake steadies the sprinkler in its new location.

WINTERIZING YOUR SYSTEM

If you live in a cold-winter climate, you must drain your irrigation system prior to the first freeze, before water frozen in pipes causes them to burst. First close the system's shutoff valve. Opening the drain valves you installed at the low points in the system will extract most of the water in the pipelines. The best way to remove any remaining water from the system is to blow compressed air through it—this is usually a job for a professional.

In milder regions where occasional freezes occur, wrap any aboveground pipes or valves, if they will contain water in winter.

Water splashing from a clogged sprinkler is wasted.

Drip systems now include microsprays, which dispense water more slowly and for shorter distances than conventional sprinklers do.

DRIP-IRRIGATION SYSTEMS

"Slow and easy" should be the motto of drip irrigation. Once known as trickle irrigation, because water dribbled or oozed out of emitters or tiny holes in plastic tubing, this form of watering is no longer restricted to dripping action. Miniature sprayers and sprinklers that put out a fraction of the water of their conventional counterparts are now part of the drip universe. Newer terminology—*low-volume irrigation* and *microirrigation*—now more accurately describes a drip system.

So slowly is moisture applied that the output rates of drip-watering devices are measured in gallons per hour (gph) rather than the gallons per minute of traditional sprinklers. If your home's water supply has a low flow rate, there's no problem—drip irrigation allows you to water a lot of plants with a scanty water source. Along with operating at low flow, a drip system operates at low pressure; most devices work best at 15 to 30 psi, though some need even lower pressure. Pressure-compensating emitters allow you to apply water uniformly, even on steep slopes.

The devices that drip or ooze water apply it near or on the ground, so there is no runoff and little or no loss to evaporation. Microsprays are not as precise as drippers and do lose water to wind and evaporation, but there's no runoff when the system is operated properly.

Drip systems are suited to all sizes of gardens, from those measured in acres to those

Water drips from a small opening in the emitter and soaks into the soil.

consisting of a few containers on a deck. Shape is no deterrent—drip works well in even or irregular areas, and in very narrow or wide spaces. Once touted as the best way to water all plants except lawn, now drip irrigation is available in an underground delivery system for turf as well (see page 81).

Originally developed for agriculture, drip systems caught on with homeowners because they're easy to put together, even for beginners. However, you can't just install a drip system and forget about it—proper scheduling and routine maintenance are essential.

Before planning a system, you'll need to know how the various components used in drip irrigation function.

BASIC COMPONENTS

Drip systems can be operated by the same kinds of control valves and timers used in underground sprinkler systems. Other drip components include filters, pressure regulators, tubing, fittings, and various types of watering devices.

CONTROL VALVES

A control valve turns the water to a circuit on and off. If you have a single drip line attached to an outdoor faucet, that faucet is your control valve. If you've attached the drip line to a battery-operated timer at the hose bibb, your control valve is built into the timer.

But if you connect directly to your water line, you'll need a separate manual or remote-control valve for each circuit. (See page 55 for general information on control valves.) Although remote-control models work at both high and low pressure, they may not close properly if the flow of water through them is too low (usually this means less than 60 gph). Generally, however, ¾-inch remote-control valves are well suited to drip systems.

When converting a conventional sprinkler circuit to drip, you can probably use the same valve. But before you rely on the valve, observe it to be sure it is shutting properly after each use. If the valve's not doing the job, turn down its flow control and choose higher-output emitters.

This remote-control antisiphon valve is connected to a Y filter and a preset pressure regulator.

BACKFLOW PREVENTERS

For a simple hose bibb system, you can use a vacuum breaker that screws onto a faucet. For a multicircuit system, you may opt for control valves that incorporate an antisiphon device, if each can be installed at least 12 inches above the highest watering device on the circuit it controls. An alternative is a single backflow preventer at the beginning of the system. For more information on types of backflow preventers, see page 39.

FILTERS

Even with municipal supplies of clean water, a filter is necessary to prevent the small openings on drip emitters and microsprays from becoming clogged. When the water source is a well, pond, or other body of water, filtration is especially important— depending on your circumstances, you may need a larger or more elaborate filter, and you'll have to clean it more often.

The screen in this Y filter can be cleaned without having to take apart the line.

Most residential drip systems use 120- to 200-mesh screen filters. The higher the mesh count, the better the screening power. In-line filters, which are often used on hose bibb systems, are the least expensive, but you have to take apart the line to wash the screen. However, on a small drip system with a clean water supply, an in-line filter may need only occasional attention. The shape of Y and T filters (which the name of each describes) allows for easy removal of the screen; some models have flush valves to further simplify cleaning.

Disk filters consist of stacks of plastic, grooved, ring-shaped disks. As water moves through them, particles are trapped in the grooves and walls. These filters are used mainly in large commercial systems or where the water comes from a pond or other algae-containing source.

PRESSURE REGULATORS

Drip systems are designed to run best at between about 15 and 30 psi, but most household water supplies have much higher pressure than that. A pressure regulator protects the fittings from blowing apart under excess force and allows the watering devices to work properly.

Most residential drip systems use plastic pressure regulators that are preset to maintain 15, 20, 25, or 30 psi. You can also obtain a version set to 10 psi for lines containing devices that work at extremely low pressure, such as ooze tubing and drip tape; this may be a good choice for lines that run downhill, as well, because water gains pressure as the elevation drops.

The various types are available with pipe threads, or with hose threads that you can screw onto a faucet or garden hose. Commercial systems often employ more expensive adjustable pressure regulators made of brass.

TUBING

Solid-walled drip tubing, or drip hose, is the standard way to distribute water from the control valve onward in a drip system. But because drip tubing isn't strong enough for lines that are under constant pressure, use buried PVC for any pipes running from the point of connection to the control valves. You may also decide in favor of running PVC beyond the valves, to get water close to your plantings, and then coming above ground with tubing. (For tubing containing regularly spaced emitters or holes, see the section on watering devices beginning on page 71.)

FERTILIZER INJECTORS

You don't need this type of device in your drip system, but you may want one. If you're accustomed to broadcasting nutrients over the soil, you should be aware that a drip system puts out too little water to dissolve the nutrients and get them down to plant roots. A fertilizer injector gets around this problem by introducing liquid or water-soluble fertilizer directly into the flowing water.

Another way to get fertilizer into the drip line is to put water-soluble tablets into your Y filter— which you'll then have to clean more often. Because just a few tablets will fit in, this method is practical only for a small circuit.

The horizontal section of this in-line fertilizer injector holds the nutrients; the vertical section is installed between the control valve (or the backflow preventer, on a hose bibb setup) and the filter.

Most drip tubing is made of polyethylene, a flexible plastic that you can cut easily with a pair of pruning shears. Resistant to ultraviolet rays from the sun, it has a life span of 15 to 25 years. The tubing is unobtrusive if covered by mulch or buried a few inches below ground.

Polyethylene tubing has "memory," meaning that it regains its normal shape after it's pushed into compression fittings or after barbed fittings are inserted into it. Thus, no glue or clamping is necessary when making connections. (For more on fittings, see below.) Drip tubing is generally sold in coils of various lengths, such as 50, 100, or 500 feet. Galvanized wire or plastic stakes are available for holding it in place.

Microtubing is joined to larger drip tubing with a barbed connector.

DRIP TUBING. Typically black, this primary conduit of drip systems can be snaked through plantings and looped around trees and shrubs, unlike rigid pipe. You can insert emitters directly into the tubing or connect them to the line via microtubing (see the photo above).

Drip tubing is sold in ½-inch and, less commonly, ⅜-inch diameters. Because both the inside and outside dimensions can vary among manufacturers, take a sample of your tubing with you as a guide when purchasing fittings and additional tubing.

MICROTUBING. Sometimes called spaghetti tubing, this small-diameter flexible pipe is used to link microsprays or individual emitters to the larger distribution line. It's commonly sold in a ¼-inch size, but ⅛-inch versions are also available. In the past, microtubing was used extensively throughout a system, creating tangles of small tubes. It tends to be used more judiciously nowadays, for specific purposes such as distributing water to containers (because it's easier to conceal than larger tubing) and attaching to the ports of multioutlet emitters (see the photo on page 72). A plastic stake is often used to hold the tubing in place, with an individual emitter or microspray at its tip.

Some types of microtubing are made from polyethylene—just like the large-diameter drip hose—and are typically available in black only. Heavyweight vinyl, which comes in several colors, is more pliable and can hug the container's shape. Be aware that not all vinyl microtubing is heavy: some kits include a thin vinyl that can easily fall out of its fittings.

To join two sections of drip tubing, push the ends into a compression coupling.

FITTINGS

These are the connectors you use when putting together a drip system. Couplings allow you to join two sections of tubing, to expand a drip circuit, or to splice damaged tubing. Tees (T shaped) let you branch off in different directions, and elbows (L shaped) are useful for making neat sharp turns, such as around deck corners. You'll find adapters to make the transition between parts with pipe threads and those with hose threads. Other fittings link tubing with PVC pipe.

To join drip tubing to a PVC tee, cement a compression adapter into the tee.

Connecting polyethylene tubing and drip fittings is easy. Instead of gluing or clamping the parts, you push them together. Three styles of fittings—compression, barbed, and locking—are available for ½- and ⅜-inch drip hose; barbed fittings are used for microtubing. With compression fittings, you shove the tubing into the fitting; with barbed fittings, you force the fitting into the tubing. Both compression and barbed types are designed to stay put once the insertion is made.

To branch a length of microtubing, cut it and force the arms of a barbed tee into the cut ends; then push another section over the tee's stem.

Either a figure-eight closure (left) or a compression end cap (right) can be used to close off the end of a drip line.

A newer style of fitting is the locking type: you insert the tubing (no force needed) and then turn a locking mechanism at the end of the fitting. People with limited strength in their hands will appreciate this type of fitting. You can also use it to make connections in drip tape—the other kinds of connectors don't fit.

End caps or figure-eight closures are used to close the ends of drip tubing. End caps, which come in both compression and locking styles, feature a tip that can be unscrewed to flush the line of sediment and other debris. End caps that flush automatically at the start and end of every watering period are also available. Figure-eight closures—you fit the tubing through one ring and then fold it back through another—are less easily removed than caps when flushing the line. Another drawback is that the folded tubing tends to deteriorate in time.

An indispensable fitting is the goof plug. Whenever you remove a drip emitter or barbed connector from the drip tubing, you just stick in one of these little plugs to keep the line from leaking.

Use a goof plug to seal a punch hole.

WATERING DEVICES

Drip irrigation was so named because that's how it applied water. Today, emitters and tubing that drip have been joined by components that spray.

DRIP EMITTERS. These devices offer a precise way to irrigate, by dripping water directly onto the soil at the plant's root zone. Most emitters have barbed ends that snap into 1/2- or 3/8-inch polyethylene tubing, or that push into the tips of microtubing linked to the larger tubing. In-line emitters are barbed on both ends so that you can create a chain of emitters. (When the factory installs in-line emitters, the resulting product is called emitter line; see page 72.)

The many emitters on the market (see an assortment at right) vary in output rate as well as shape, size, and internal mechanism—the way the emitter slows down the flow of water so that it drips out. Most types dispense

Be sure to insert the barbed end of the emitter, not the end that drips water, into the drip tubing.

1/2, 1, or 2 gph, and manufacturers usually color-code the emitters to make their output obvious at a glance. An emitter's size and shape is related partly to the internal mechanism, partly to marketing considerations.

Here's how the various internal mechanisms work. *Vortex* emitters decelerate water by spinning it out from the center. In a *laminar-flow* emitter, water slows down as it travels through a corkscrew pattern set in a straight path. *Turbulent-flow* emitters send water through a circular maze; the wide channels allow larger particulates through, making this emitter less likely to clog than vortex or laminar-flow types. *Diaphragm* emitters have a flexible opening that changes size at different pressure levels; this makes them pressure compensating and generally self cleaning.

Various internal mechanisms slow the water so that it emerges in drips.

Your choice of emitter type will depend on your terrain, the length of your drip lines, and your water quality. All types work well on relatively level ground and for lines less than 200 feet long. But if your surface varies in elevation by more than 10 vertical feet or your line exceeds 200 feet, choose diaphragm (usually sold as "pressure-compensating") emitters: they will deliver the same amount of water throughout the line. If your water contains pollutants that can clog the emitters, your best bet is a turbulent-flow or diaphragm type. With all types, the emitters with the lowest output rates have the smallest drip openings and are more prone to clogging than their larger-gallonage counterparts.

Some emitters are adjustable. By turning a cap, you can change the output from droplets to a gentle stream. Set on the upper end of the output range (up to 20 gph on some types), these emitters—sometimes called bubblers—are especially useful for spreading water throughout the root zone of plants growing in very sandy soils in the ground or in porous container mixes. If dispensed in drips, the water would tend to go straight down, without much sideways movement.

Other special emitters act as hubs—they contain up to 12 outlets, or ports, from which you run microtubing

PUNCHES

These tools are used to make small barb-size holes in drip tubing. Most punches require that you pierce the hose first and then insert the emitter barb. With some types, you place the emitter on the tool so that the barb is implanted as you punch.

You can attach microtubing to each outlet of a multioutlet emitter.

to nearby plants. Types that put out about the same amount of water per outlet as standard emitters do are generally referred to as multioutlet emitters. But when the outlets are rated at higher gallonages, they are typically called bubblers; sometimes each outlet will have a different flow rate, or the outlets may be made adjustable by turning little valves or substituting different inserts. Multioutlet emitters are available with a barb to attach to drip tubing or with an adapter to screw onto a conventional sprinkler riser (see page 84 for information on converting sprinklers to drip).

EMITTER LINE. This is standard ½-inch drip tubing or ¼-inch microtubing, but with emitters already installed at regular intervals along its length. Sturdy and long lasting, emitter line is less expensive than tubing and in-line emitters bought separately. It waters more evenly over a longer length than do other types of soakers, including laser tubing and soaker hose (see below).

You can lay the larger-diameter emitter line in parallel rows in a densely planted area like a vegetable garden, or on either side of closely spaced plants like a hedge. The smaller emitter line is well suited to window boxes and large containers.

The ½-inch version is available with ½-, 1-, or 2-gph emitters spaced 12, 18, 24, or 36 inches apart (½-gph emitters 12 inches apart is the most common arrangement). The microemitter line has ½-gph emitters spaced 6 or 12 inches apart.

The emitters are typically either turbulent-flow or pressure-compensating (diaphragm) types. Turbulent-flow emit-

The winding chambers of this in-line emitter are normally hidden from view.

ters are suitable for most situations; because of their wide channels, they rarely clog. Pressure-compensating emitters are preferred on slopes or hilly terrain, or for especially long lines.

Emitter line for underground drip systems (see page 81) is the same as the type used above ground, except that the emitters may be treated with an herbicide to keep grass roots out.

LASER TUBING. This ¼-inch polyethylene tubing has laser-drilled holes at regular intervals (usually every 6 or 12 inches). You close the end of the line with a goof plug. Laser tubing is more prone to clogging and shorter-lived than emitter line, but it costs less. Arrows along the length of the tubing indicate the direction in which the water should flow.

OOZE TUBING. This type of soaker hose—available in ½- and ¼-inch diameters—can be incorporated into a drip circuit. It works best when the pressure is 10 psi, when it is laid on fairly flat ground, and when each line is kept short (a maximum of 50 feet for the ½-inch type, 15 feet for the smaller one). For more on ooze tubing, see page 51.

DRIP TAPE. Used mainly in agriculture, this inexpensive polyethylene product must be used on fairly level terrain, laid in straight rows, and secured at the ends to keep it from twisting. It doesn't contain drip emitters, but rather internal flow paths that slow the water down so it emerges in drips from regularly spaced openings. Typically operated at 10 psi, it needs special fittings.

A roll of drip tape with some of its special fittings

TOP: Emitter line contains factory-installed in-line drip emitters spaced at set intervals.

MIDDLE: Be sure to lay laser tubing so that water flows in the direction of the arrows. It will drip out through the regularly spaced laser-drilled holes.

BOTTOM: A compression tee joins ½-inch drip tubing with similarly sized ooze tubing.

Drip tape comes in several weights—the heavier, the longer lasting. For example, 4- and 8-mil types are disposed of after one season, whereas 15-mil tape can be reused for several.

MICROSPRAYS. These look like miniature versions of conventional sprinklers, and some are even available on little pop-up risers. They discharge more water than do drip emitters, but they apply it less precisely—and some of it is lost to evaporation. However, microsprays irrigate a larger area than drippers do, so you need far fewer of them to cover the same planting.

Their larger droplets make minisprinklers less subject to wind drift than minisprays.

They're useful for irrigating closely spaced or dense plantings, such as ground covers and flower beds, and for dispensing water over the root zones of trees and shrubs. You wouldn't substitute microsprays for conventional lawn sprinklers, though, because you'd have to run them for many hours to get the same amount of water to the root zone.

As with standard sprinklers, the sprays from these low-volume heads should be overlapped for good coverage (see page 59). Because the spray consists of fewer droplets, it is more subject to wind drift than the heavier spray from conventional sprinklers. As plants grow, microsprays may have to be repositioned or elevated if their spray is blocked.

This minispray dispenses water in a bow tie pattern.

Minisprays. These little heads are available in various spray patterns, including quarter, half, and full circles, as well as a bow tie shape. Output ranges from about 6 to 30 gph and the radius of throw from about 4 to 10 feet. They're useful for covering tight or irregular spaces.

Minisprinklers. Also called spinners, these devices cover larger areas than minisprays can, throwing water in circles measuring from about 10 to 30 feet across. Because the spray consists of larger droplets than that of minisprays, it is less affected by wind. Output ranges from about 6 to 50 gph.

Misters. To raise the humidity around plants like fuchsias, tuberous begonias, bromeliads, and ferns, or to water hanging plants and bonsai, choose misters. They are usually positioned above hanging plants, so that the spray is directed downward; for in-ground plants, they are generally positioned so that they spray upward.

A mister over a hanging basket keeps plants evenly moist.

TIMERS

An optional timer, or controller, lets you automate your watering. A battery-operated model attached to the faucet will suffice for a simple hose bibb system. If your irrigation system is divided into several circuits, whether all drip or partly conventional sprinkler circuits, choose a multistation timer. For more information, see the section beginning on page 85.

For more information, see the section beginning on page 85.

DRIP KITS VERSUS CUSTOM COMPONENTS

If you've never put in a drip system before, you may be tempted to buy a kit rather than plan your own system and obtain all the parts on your own.

Some kits provide the preassembled parts for hooking up to a hose bibb or garden hose, for connecting to an irrigation control valve, or for converting a conventional sprinkler head to drip. Other kits provide drip tubing and drip emitters or microsprays in sufficient quantity to water a certain number of plants or a certain square footage of planting area. Some suppliers gear each kit to a particular planting type, such as vegetable garden, rose garden, or container plants.

Kits may be convenient, especially if you have only a few plants or a small area to water, but they can also be constraining. Note that some kits come with a flow control device rather than an actual pressure regulator—the system may not work properly if you use only a few of the emitters that come with the kit, or if you add extra ones. A system that you put together yourself will fit your garden and do exactly what you want it to do. Buying the parts individually is also less expensive than getting them in kit form.

Keep in mind that assembling a drip system is relatively easy, even for beginners, so there's no reason to settle for a kit if it doesn't precisely serve your needs.

Planning your system

A drip system can be as simple or elaborate as you like—anything from a single short line connected to the end of a garden hose to a multicircuit system cut into your house service line and wired to a timer. Your piping may be flexible tubing placed on the soil surface or a network of buried PVC pipes—just as in an underground sprinkler system—to which you connect drip components above ground. You can stick with a single type of watering device—such as drip emitters, microsprays, or emitter line—or incorporate various types in your system.

The following discussion summarizes the steps to take in planning a drip system. If you've never designed one before, don't agonize over it—drip systems leave room for error and mind-changing. If you find that you've located drip tubing in the wrong place, just pick up the line and move it. Even if rigid underground pipe ends up a few feet away from its ideal location, extra tubing from the riser will span the difference. If you discover that you didn't allocate enough emitters to wet a plant's root zone, add more emitters. If you decide that microsprays would do a better job than emitters, switch to them.

SELECTING WATERING DEVICES

To specify the type and number of emitters for your garden, you'll need a copy of the scale drawing of your property divided into hydrozones (see page 53). Your task is to assign watering devices to each area that will be covered by your drip system. You may have firm ideas about which devices to use—perhaps emitter line for your vegetable garden and individual emitters for a shrub bed. If you're undecided, consult the chapter beginning on page 97 for recommendations on drip-irrigation devices suitable for each planting type.

Microsprays provide perfect coverage for this narrow bed of lettuce nestled between house and path.

Also keep the following guidelines in mind. Individual drip emitters are useful for watering widely spaced plants, whereas emitter line and microsprays are suited to closely spaced plants. You may opt for emitter line if you want to keep the foliage dry, but microsprays if your soil is very porous. And emitter line, ooze tubing, and shorter-lived products like drip tape and laser tubing are all appropriate for watering rows of plants.

Note on your scale drawing the category of watering device you want for each hydrozone. Also note where any pressure-compensating emitters are needed (on hilly areas). For individual drip emitters, refer to the chart on the facing page to determine the output rate and number of emitters that you'll need per plant.

DRIP-EMITTER WETTING PATTERNS

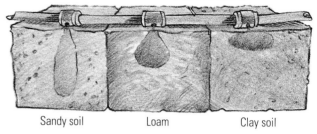

Sandy soil   Loam   Clay soil

The number of drip emitters required depends not just on the size of the plant but also on your soil. To compensate for water's lack of lateral movement in sandy soil, you'll need more drippers than in loam or clay soils.

Use a pencil compass to sketch in the spray patterns of any microsprays you've selected. Even though these little sprinklers and spray heads throw water for a shorter distance than conventional sprinklers do, use the same principles for laying them out (see page 59). Use the fewest number of heads that will cover the area, and overlap the sprays. You don't have to be as precise as you would be in laying out standard sprinklers, because it's easy to alter microspray locations and to add or subtract heads. Refer to the chart on the facing page for some common microspray throw distances and output rates.

ASSIGNING WATERING DEVICES

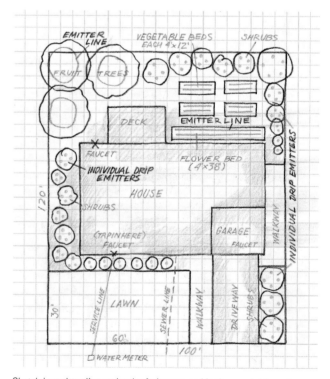

Sketch in emitter line under the fruit trees and in the vegetable and flower beds. Also mark individual emitters for the shrub plantings, using the chart on the facing page as a guide. If there were microsprays, you would draw them in too.

DRIP-EMITTER SELECTION GUIDE

This list provides general guidelines for the number and gallonage of emitters for various types of plantings. The goal is to wet at least 60 percent of the root zone, so you may need to make adjustments depending on your soil type. Water tends to drip mainly downward in sandy soils but spread wider before it goes deep in loam and clay soils (see the illustration on the facing page). Wherever a range is given for the number of emitters, choose the higher number if your soil is sandy, the lower number if it's clayey. You may need more emitters of a lower gallonage for plants on a slope, to avoid runoff.

	OUTPUT RATE	NUMBER OF EMITTERS	PLACEMENT
Vegetables, closely spaced	1/2–1 gph	1	every 12 inches
Vegetables, widely spaced	1–2 gph	1	at base of plant
Flower beds	1 gph	1	at base of plant
Ground covers	1 gph	1	at base of plant
Shrubs (2–3 ft.)	1 gph	1–2	at base of plant
Shrubs and trees (3–5 ft.)	1 gph	2	6–12 inches on either side
Shrubs and trees (5–10 ft.)	2 gph	2–3	2 feet from trunk
Shrubs and trees (10–20 ft.)	2 gph	3–4	3 feet apart, at drip line
Trees (over 20 ft.)	2 gph	6 or more	4 feet apart, at drip line

MICROSPRAY SELECTION GUIDE

Many microsprays are adjustable or offer a selection of nozzles, so you're bound to find types that will adequately cover the areas you wish to irrigate. Here is a sampling of arcs, radius distances, and output rates, to help you lay out the heads.

FULL CIRCLE	HALF CIRCLE	QUARTER CIRCLE	BOW TIE	OUTPUT RATE
8 ft.	5 ft.	5 ft.	4 ft.	6 gph
9 ft.	6 ft.	6 ft.	5 ft.	10 gph
11 ft.	7 ft.	7 ft.	6 ft.	17 gph
12 ft.	8 ft.	8 ft.	7 ft.	24 gph

PLOTTING CIRCUITS

Your system may have a single circuit or several circuits—that is, groups of watering devices controlled by the same valve. You may have to break your system up into two or more circuits so that plants with different moisture needs or those that grow in different soil types can be watered separately. Another reason for additional circuits is to avoid allocating more water to a circuit than you have available.

On the other hand, there are ways to avoid adding circuits. You can use an in-line shutoff valve to control flow to one section of a circuit that needs less water than the rest of the line does— for example, in the case of native plants that will be watered less and less frequently over time. Or, if you have a small garden of plants that share fairly similar watering requirements, you can get away with a single circuit by adding extra or higher-gallonage emitters to take care of the thirstier or larger plants.

You have a lot more leeway in plotting circuits for a drip system than for an underground sprinkler system—partly because you can mix types of watering devices on one circuit (for example, drip emitters, microsprays, and soaker hoses) and partly

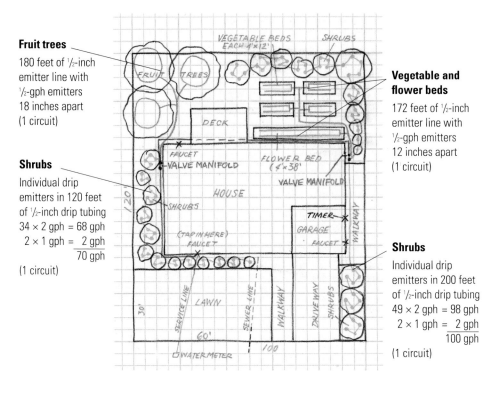

Fruit trees

180 feet of ½-inch emitter line with ½-gph emitters 18 inches apart (1 circuit)

Shrubs

Individual drip emitters in 120 feet of ½-inch drip tubing
34 × 2 gph = 68 gph
2 × 1 gph = 2 gph
70 gph
(1 circuit)

Vegetable and flower beds

172 feet of ½-inch emitter line with ½-gph emitters 12 inches apart (1 circuit)

Shrubs

Individual drip emitters in 200 feet of ½-inch drip tubing
49 × 2 gph = 98 gph
2 × 1 gph = 2 gph
100 gph
(1 circuit)

To plot circuits, add up the gallonage of individual emitters (see the chart on page 75) and calculate the length of emitter line (see the chart on the facing page). In the sample plan, the fruit trees can be on one circuit, the vegetable and flower beds on another, and the shrubs on two additional circuits—for a total of four circuits.

The emitter line or individual drip emitters in each circuit will be connected with drip tubing, which should lead to a valve controlling that circuit. To keep the drip tubing within allowable length limits, valves for the fruit trees and one shrub circuit are located on the left side of the house, with the lawn sprinkler valve (see page 62). The valves for the remaining shrubs and the vegetable and flower bed circuits are positioned on the right side of the house. Extend the irrigation main line from the valve manifold on the left side around the house to the second manifold.

---

because drip devices put out so little water in comparison. You do have to pay more attention to how many devices you use on microtubing than on larger drip tubing, and when using some of the higher-gallonage sprays. You can write down the gph of each microspray next to it, but don't bother doing that with a large number of drip emitters. Instead, just note the number of each gallonage type.

Total the output (in gph) of all the watering devices in a circuit. You should be safe if you keep within the flow guidelines for the various tubing types and sizes listed in the chart on the facing page.

You will have to connect all the watering devices on a circuit to the same drip line (leading back to the valve), so they should be in the same vicinity. Don't worry about showing the exact location of drip emitters on your plan—that's something you'll determine mainly during installation.

LOCATING THE CONTROL VALVES AND TIMER

For a simple hose bibb drip system, the outdoor faucet—or a battery-operated timer attached to the faucet—will serve as your valve.

For a multicircuit system, you can install a separate valve at the beginning of the circuit it operates, or you can cluster the valves in a manifold—the latter will ease the task of wiring the valves to the timer. In addition to marking the location of each valve on your

plan, also note where the timer will go—usually it will be indoors, near an electrical outlet.

LAYING OUT THE TUBING

Draw lines that represent drip tubing connecting the various watering devices in each circuit to the control valve for that circuit. Note the length of tubing and the number and types of fittings needed. For in-ground plants, minimize the use of microtubing by connecting emitters directly to the drip tubing. Too much microtubing in the garden is a nuisance, tripping people and snagging rakes and other garden tools. For a container planting, run the low-profile microtubing from the lateral line up into each pot. Rather than weaving a single long line of drip hose back and forth across a slope, run a supply line downhill and tee off laterals with emitters across the slope.

ASSEMBLING A SHOPPING LIST

Referring to your scale drawing, total the number of control valves, the numbers and types of fittings and watering devices, and the total length of each type of tubing or pipe. To determine the length of low-voltage wire to connect the control valves to the timer, see page 87. Don't forget to include a punch tool on your list.

You'd be wise to buy extra emitters, fittings (especially connectors and goof plugs), and tubing. That way, you'll be able to make alterations and repairs as needed.

KEEPING MAXIMUMS IN MIND

For proper operation of your drip system, try to keep within the recommended flow limits for drip tubing, emitter line, and laser tubing.

DRIP TUBING

The chart below indicates the maximum flow rate for the various sizes and types of drip tubing. Add up the gallonage of all the watering devices connected to the tubing, to be sure you don't exceed the flow rate.

For best performance, also heed the maximum recommended tubing length, though you can exceed those figures somewhat if you are using pressure-compensating emitters.

	DIAMETER	MAXIMUM FLOW RATE	MAXIMUM LENGTH
Polyethylene tubing	$\frac{1}{2}$ in.	320 gph	200 ft.
	$\frac{3}{8}$ in.	100 gph	100 ft.
	$\frac{1}{4}$ in.	15 gph	25 ft.
	$\frac{1}{8}$ in.	4 gph	10 ft.
Heavyweight vinyl	$\frac{1}{4}$ in.	12 gph	20 ft.

EMITTER LINE

The following are suggested maximum runs for commonly used emitter line incorporating turbulent-flow emitters. You can run lines a bit longer when using emitter line with pressure-compensating emitters.

TUBING DIAMETER	OUTPUT RATE	EMITTER SPACING	MAXIMUM LENGTH
$\frac{1}{2}$ in.	$\frac{1}{2}$ gph	12 in. apart	200 ft.
$\frac{1}{2}$ in.	$\frac{1}{2}$ gph	18 in. apart	260 ft.
$\frac{1}{2}$ in.	$\frac{1}{2}$ gph	24 in. apart	320 ft.
$\frac{1}{4}$ in.	$\frac{1}{2}$ gph	6 in. apart	15 ft.
$\frac{1}{4}$ in.	$\frac{1}{2}$ gph	12 in. apart	25 ft.

LASER TUBING

For the most uniform watering, keep to within the maximum lengths listed below.

TUBING DIAMETER	OUTPUT RATE	SLIT SPACING	MAXIMUM LENGTH
$\frac{1}{4}$ in.	1 gph	6 in. apart	10 ft.
$\frac{1}{4}$ in.	1 gph	12 in. apart	15 ft.

IN-LINE SHUTOFF VALVES

You may decide to incorporate manual shutoff valves in your lines to isolate portions of circuits. These handy devices are sold in $\frac{1}{2}$-, $\frac{3}{8}$-, and $\frac{1}{4}$-inch sizes to fit the corresponding size of tubing; similar devices in various sizes are available for PVC lines. They allow you to turn off water to a particular section and then turn it back on when you want to irrigate. For example, you may want to turn off water to a segment of the vegetable garden that lies fallow for part of the year.

An in-line shutoff valve controls the flow of water to this raised bed.

INSTALLING YOUR SYSTEM

Because drip systems are made up of a lot of little parts, organizing them by size and type will make installation go more smoothly. Put all of the compression couplings, barbed connectors, different gallonage emitters, and other components into separate containers—plastic zip bags, for example.

Once you've sorted the parts, you're ready to begin the actual installation. The most efficient procedure is to start with the head assembly and then position the water-distribution lines. After clearing the lines of any debris, you can install all of the watering devices. Because of the flexibility of a drip system, you can reposition lines and add or subtract drip emitters and microsprays, if necessary, as you go along.

The smallest, simplest systems should go very rapidly. Don't feel obliged to install a larger, multicircuit system all at once, if you have only a few hours here and there to devote to the task—do it in stages.

CONSTRUCTING THE HEAD ASSEMBLY

Rather than just the control valve (and perhaps antisiphon valve) that marks the beginning of an underground sprinkler circuit, several components are required at the start of a low-pressure, low-volume drip circuit. These components—control valve, backflow preventer, filter, pressure regulator, and optional fertilizer injector—are known collectively as the head assembly, or valve assembly. (A backflow preventer in the head assembly is unnecessary if one for the whole system is located at the point of connection or in the irrigation main line; see page 39.)

For a multicircuit drip system you could have a single filter and pressure regulator in the irrigation main leading to several circuits' valves, but you'd have to buy a larger filter, strong enough to withstand constant pressure, and a brass adjustable pressure regulator. In many cases, a separate filter and pressure regulator in each circuit's head assembly is more economical.

There are two types of head assemblies: a hose-thread head assembly and a pipe-thread head assembly. Be sure to get components with the appropriate threads, because forcing incompatible types together will strip the threads.

HOSE-THREAD HEAD ASSEMBLY. The easiest way to connect a simple system to your water supply is to screw it onto an outdoor faucet, or even onto a garden hose. You may want to attach your system to one branch of a hose-Y, leaving the faucet free for other uses.

For the head assembly, choose components that have hose threads, so that they are compatible with the threads on the faucet or garden hose. Hose-thread parts are lighter than pipe-thread ones and will carry less flow, so be sure that all the watering devices on the circuit combined don't exceed the maximum flow rate for the part.

To automate the system, screw a battery-operated timer on first, followed by a vacuum breaker, filter, pressure regulator, and thread-to-tubing compression adapter (you insert the drip tubing into it). An optional fertilizer injector goes between the vacuum breaker and filter—you don't need the individual vacuum breaker if your injector has one built in.

You can use an in-line filter if your circuit is small and your water supply has few impurities, because you probably won't have to remove it for cleaning very often. Y and T filters are more appropriate for larger circuits; because you don't have to dismantle them for cleaning, they're convenient if you anticipate frequent flushings.

Hose-thread components naturally screw together in the proper direction, so there's no chance of assembling any part backward. The washers in hose-thread parts should seal properly when the

Depending on the type and number of components in your drip system, installation can go very quickly. This emitter line setup, put in just before planting, was especially easy because the emitters are factory installed.

Both of these hose-thread head assemblies will screw directly onto an outdoor faucet. The one on the left has a simple mechanical timer and in-line filter, whereas the one on the right has a battery-operated timer and Y filter. Both include a preset pressure regulator and a thread-to-tubing compression adapter.

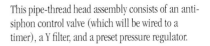

parts are hand tightened; don't use a wrench. Brace or otherwise protect the assembly if it's heavy or sticks out so far that it's in danger of being kicked.

PIPE-THREAD HEAD ASSEMBLY. This type of assembly is plumbed into a water supply pipe. The circuit typically begins with a control valve—often combined with an antisiphon device—wired to a timer.

The pipe-thread components screw together: wrap the threads with pipe-thread tape before hand-tightening (you can use a wrench, but do so gently). Be sure to assemble the parts with the arrows pointing in the direction of water flow. Attach a Y or T filter, then a pressure regulator, and finally a thread-to-tubing adapter. If you opt for a fertilizer injector, install it between the valve and filter.

This pipe-thread head assembly consists of an anti-siphon control valve (which will be wired to a timer), a Y filter, and a preset pressure regulator.

TUBING TRICKS

Bring out your drip tubing early and leave it in the sun—the softened material will fit into compression fittings more easily. If the tubing feels stiff on a cold or overcast day, try soaking the end in warm water. Never use soap or any lubricant, such as grease or oil, to force the drip hose in.

To make insertions easy, scribe a line with your thumbnail about ½ inch from the end. Then push the tubing in, stopping at the line. Pushed in too far, the tubing can interfere with water flow.

LAYING THE LINES

Start laying the water-distribution line from the head assembly, working toward the plants to be irrigated. Insert the drip hose into the compression adapter at the end of the assembly. (If you're starting the line with buried PVC pipe, see page 64 for information on working with that material.)

Lay drip tubing for the whole circuit, following the plan you sketched. To avoid kinking the tubing, unroll it as you go, rather than pulling off coils. You'll probably have to anchor it in the ground at intervals with galvanized wire or plastic stakes. Be sure to leave a little slack in the line, to allow for the tubing to expand in hot weather and contract in cold.

Unroll drip tubing as you go.

If you need to make an acute turn, cut the tubing with pruning shears or a sharp utility knife and rejoin the ends with an elbow. To branch the line, cut it and rejoin the pieces in the arms of a tee; insert additional drip hose or emitter line in the stem of the tee. Because emitter line and other soakers combine tubing with the watering devices, you can lay them now or wait until you install the emitters and microsprays. Try to keep dirt out of the tubing as you work.

Elbows allow for neat, sharp turns.

If you need to lay drip hose under a walkway, use the method described on page 63. If you buy the kit containing the power nozzle, use the length of PVC as a sleeve for the drip tubing.

FLUSHING THE SYSTEM

Before installing the watering devices, you must flush the drip lines of dirt and debris. Once the water runs clear from the ends of the lines, you can turn off the water and close the lines. Either cap the ends (by inserting the tubing into a compression fitting with a screw cap), or fit them into a figure-eight closure.

INSTALLING WATERING DEVICES

Use your plan as a guide in locating the various watering devices—but don't hesitate to reposition drip emitters and other devices as dictated by the actual conditions you encounter.

Secure drip tubing every so often with a landscape stake like this plastic type. Once the tubing is in place, you can camouflage it with decorative rocks or other materials.

This type of punch implants the emitter's barb directly into the tubing as you punch. Place the emitter into the end of the tool and punch, heeding the pointers in the box above.

PUNCHING POINTERS

When making holes in drip tubing for emitters and barbed fittings, use a punch designed for that purpose. Be sure the tubing is lying straight—if it's twisted, the emitter could end up on top, causing water to run along the tubing instead of dripping down onto the soil. The hole should be positioned so that the emitter will drip to the side or downward.

Hold the punch at a right angle to the tubing to ensure a round hole that will seal tightly against the emitter's barb. You may find the piercing process to be easier if you slowly twist the punch as you push it into the tubing. On some punches, the tip may become clogged with extracted tubing; clear it out before punching again.

For a neat, well-placed hole, position the punch at a right angle to the tubing.

DRIP EMITTERS. To install a drip emitter directly into ½- or ⅜-inch drip tubing, punch a hole in the tubing and then insert the barbed end of the emitter (or use a punch that inserts the emitter directly). If you punch a hole in the wrong place, seal it with a goof plug.

Another way to install an emitter is at the tip of microtubing that you run from the drip hose to the plant. Insert a barbed connector (or tee, if you want emitters at the tips of two short lines) into one end of the microtubing and insert it into a hole you've punched in the drip hose. Push the emitter into the other end of the microtubing and position it at the plant—it's usually mounted on a special stake designed for that purpose. A multioutlet emitter works basically the same way: you run microtubing from each of the barbed ports out to plants. (To install a multioutlet emitter onto a conventional sprinkler riser, see page 84.)

To make a chain of in-line emitters, insert the barb on each end of the emitters into microtubing, spacing the emitters as desired. Then attach this homemade "emitter line" to the drip tubing with a single barbed connector.

Regardless of how you install the emitters, be sure to position them so that they deliver water evenly to plant roots. Also take care to set them away from the stems of woody plants, to avoid rot. For new plantings of all kinds, drip emitters must be placed so that they drip directly on the root ball. On slopes, locate emitters on the uphill side of the plants.

A microtubing support stake will hold the emitter in place near the plant.

MICROSPRAYS. These little sprayers can be installed in various ways. A common method is to punch a hole in the drip tubing and insert a rigid microspray riser—you screw the head onto the riser top. If the tubing twists, however, the riser and head will tilt, causing the water to be misdirected.

Continued on page 82 >

Underground Drip for Lawns

Lawns can now be watered by drip, thanks to advancements in emitter line technology. One manufacturer infuses the emitters with herbicide, to keep grass roots from growing into the openings. Other makers say that proper operation of the system is enough to discourage clogging.

The primary benefit of an underground drip system is water conservation, because no moisture is lost to evaporation, runoff, or overshooting lawn boundaries. The drippers also deliver water more uniformly than sprinklers do. The system is especially useful where sprinklers don't do a good job, such as in irregularly shaped or very narrow strips of lawn. It's not really suited to large areas.

Underground drip isn't advised for very porous or gravelly soils, where the lateral movement of water is restricted, or for lawns containing many tree roots. Also, installing it in soil infested with gophers or other burrowing creatures is chancy.

If you're an old hand at drip irrigation, you'll probably want to tackle the installation of this system yourself. However, if you have little or no experience with drip, you are better off employing the services of a professional.

SETTING UP A SYSTEM

The basic design consists of parallel emitter lines; see a typical layout at right. Soil type determines the spacing between the lines, as well as the spacing between emitters and the output of each emitter. The lighter the soil, the tighter the spacing and the higher the gallonage rate, because the water won't spread as far laterally as it would in heavier soils. Thus, in sandy soil, you'd choose 1-gph emitters spaced at 12-inch intervals, with lines 14 to 16 inches apart; in clay soil, you could manage with ½-gph emitters spaced every 18 inches, with lines separated by 18 inches. On a slope, the lines should be placed about 25 percent closer together at the top and 25 percent farther apart at the bottom. Lines should also be placed no farther than 4 inches from walkways or other hard edges, to prevent dry strips.

In the illustration below, PVC headers (in this case, ¾-inch pipe) connect the polyethylene emitter lines on both ends, with a series of slip (unthreaded) elbows and tees. The fittings are the same diameter as the header pipe on one end of the elbows and on both arms of the tees; the other end of the elbows and the stem end of the tees should be ½ inch in diameter, the size of the emitter line. A compression fitting adapter cemented to the inside of each fitting turns it into a drip compression fitting. The tubing will hold when pushed into the fitting.

An automatic flush valve, which should be protected in a valve box, is connected to the header farthest from the water supply. Its purpose is to allow any debris to escape from the tubing every time the circuit turns on and off.

If you don't use an anti-siphon valve at the beginning of the circuit, you should install an air relief valve at the highest point—it operates while the system is draining, allowing air to replace water in the tubing, and thus helps prevent the suction of sediment into the emitters.

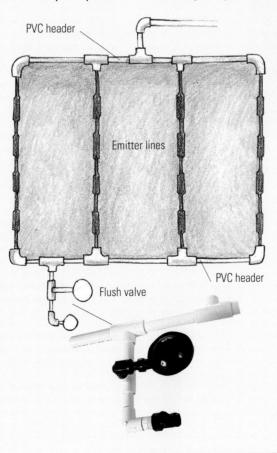

PVC header

Emitter lines

Flush valve

PVC header

A standard layout consists of parallel emitter lines connected to PVC headers. An automatic flush valve (which should be protected in a valve box) helps keep the lines clear of any debris.

Another option is to punch a hole and insert a barbed connector joining a short length of microtubing from the larger tubing to a stake. Some stakes are intended for support only—you secure the spray head to the top in some sort of holder. Other types allow you to screw the head directly onto the stake.

Yet another alternative is a combination stake-and-riser unit, with a barbed insert on the side of the stake. You simply push the stake into the ground, then insert the barb into a hole you punch in the side of the drip tubing, and finally screw the microspray head onto the riser top.

To address the problem of risers snapping off or being knocked over, some companies now offer pop-ups for microsprays—they connect to microtubing, just as the other devices do. These pop-up microsprays are visible only when they're actually spraying water.

If you designed a system of buried PVC pipes, you can opt to attach the microspray to a special riser that screws directly into PVC fittings.

EMITTER LINE. Join ½-inch emitter line to the drip tubing with a compression fitting (a tee, elbow, or coupling, as determined by the layout). A barbed connector will link ¼-inch emitter line to the drip tubing.

INSTALLING THE TIMER

Simple hose bibb systems generally employ a battery-operated timer attached to the faucet before the head assembly. But if you have several circuits (whether all drip or a combination of drip and conventional sprinklers), you'll need to install a timer, or controller, and wire your remote-control valves to it. For information on these steps, see the section beginning on page 85.

TESTING THE SYSTEM

After turning on the water to the irrigation system at the shutoff valve, switch on each circuit manually at the timer. If none of the circuits of a multicircuit system comes on, inspect the remote-control valves to be sure they were installed in the right direction, with the arrow pointing in the direction of the water flow. If that's not the problem, check the wiring at the valves and the controller. If only one circuit fails to come on, check the flow control setting at that particular valve.

Once water is flowing through the lines, look for any leaks. If you left any open holes in the tubing, insert goof plugs. If tubing has been accidentally gashed, cut out that piece and put in a compression coupling. A failure of any individual emitters or microsprays to put out water probably means they're clogged from debris that was in the line. Remove the emitter or sprayer and clean it. Also examine all the watering devices to be sure they're properly positioned near their plants. Move them as needed, plugging their holes in the tubing. Adjust the microsprays' direction or throw as required.

Once you're happy with the system, you can cover the tubing with mulch.

TOP: Microtubing topped by a microspray is attached to a support stake.

BOTTOM: A microspray is being screwed directly into the top of a stake designed for that purpose.

Water spurting from a hole originally made for a barbed connector is easily sealed with a goof plug.

MAINTAINING YOUR SYSTEM

Regular maintenance is the key to keeping a drip system in good working order. You can divide that maintenance into three categories: the type needed at the beginning of the growing season, ongoing upkeep during the season, and preparing the system for winter.

STARTING THE SEASON RIGHT

Check the entire system before the first use of the year—and at least once during each season in which the system is in operation, if you live in a mild-winter region. If your water contains sediment or hard minerals, check the system more often.

Before the first use of the season, open the end caps and run the water for 2 to 5 minutes to wash accumulated sediment out of the lines. Flush the lines every 4 to 6 months if your water is fairly clean, more often if it isn't.

Check the emitters after the first couple of uses at the start of the season. Be sure that water is flowing through them and that the wetting pattern is what you expected. If an emitter isn't dripping water, pull it out and clean it. If that doesn't do the trick, replace it with a new emitter.

REMAINING ALERT

Make sure your filters are clean—if you have a clean municipal water supply, you may find that yearly cleaning is more than sufficient. If your water is high in sediment, on the other hand, check the filters frequently. To clean an in-line filter, remove its screen and wash it under running water; replace a damaged or torn screen. You don't have to take apart the line to clean the screen of a Y or T filter; just unscrew the cap and remove the filter. Some have flush valves that allow you to clean the screen in place.

Check the system periodically while it is running. Look for any clogged emitters or microsprays. Clogging is more of a problem where the water source contains hard minerals or other contaminants that come out of solution when exposed to air. If you can't clear the clog, install a new emitter or spray head.

Look for leaks: puddles, miniature geysers, and eroded soil are clues. Sometimes they're caused by connections pulling apart (repair them) or emitters becoming dislodged (pop them back in place). Secure any tubing that has come loose from its stake.

If your water source is well water or gray water, be aware that algae can build up. To eliminate it, flush the drip system with granular chlorine (not liquid chlorine, which may harm plants) or other products made for that purpose.

Adapt the drip system to your garden as it evolves. Move emitters farther away from a plant's base as the roots grow and add emitters if needed. If expanding foliage blocks spray, reposition the microspray or extend its riser.

WINTERIZING YOUR SYSTEM

In a freezing climate, you must protect your drip system. Remove the end caps to allow the lines to drain. Turn off the water supply to the irrigation system. Unscrew any head assemblies attached to hose bibbs or garden hoses and drain any Y or T filters, which may have water in them. Bring the entire assembly indoors.

If you can take up your drip lines without permanently tangling them or losing the watering devices, store them indoors. After reinstalling the lines in spring, flush them as you did when first installing the system.

You can leave the lines in place if you've drained them and removed their end closures. Burying the lines under heavy mulch for the winter will protect them. Be sure to flush the lines before using the system again in the spring.

If freezes are only occasional in your area, wrap any aboveground pipes or valves that will contain water in winter.

This T filter has a flush valve that makes it easy to clean its screen.

Periodically inspect emitters to be sure they're dispensing water properly. If you were to detect a problem with any individual emitter connected to this multioutlet unit positioned below ground, you would have to remove the protective cover and check the attachment of the microtubing to the ports.

CONVERTING TO DRIP

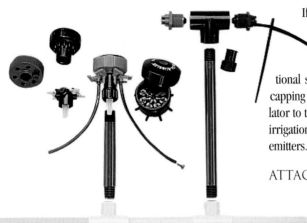

If some circuits on your conventional sprinkler system are watering plants that could be irrigated more efficiently with drip, you can retrofit the system, making use of the existing underground pipes.

The various conversion methods call for removing all of the conventional sprinklers on a circuit, connecting drip components at one or more risers, and capping all risers that aren't used. In most cases, you must add a filter and a pressure regulator to the line. You'll probably be able to use the same control valve, but check with your irrigation supplier to make sure. To be on the safe side, avoid using the lowest-gallonage emitters.

ATTACHING MULTIOUTLET EMITTERS

Screw multioutlet emitters directly onto the risers. This type of emitter has a built-in pressure regulator and filter—as long as your water pressure is less than 80 psi and your water source is clean, you won't need an additional pressure regulator and filter. See page 71 for more on these devices.

Because multioutlet emitters act as hubs, they are most useful in small gardens and wherever plants are clustered around the risers.

CONNECTING AT ONE RISER

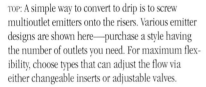

This system is best used in a simple, linear planting area such as a parking strip or flower bed. It makes use of one central sprinkler on the line. The most common connection is an elbow that is screwed onto the riser and to which you attach a filter, pressure regulator, and compression adapter to accept drip tubing or emitter line.

As an alternative to that connection technique, one manufacturer makes a pop-up body that will accept an internal assembly containing a pressure regulator and filter. The assembly, which you drop into the sprinkler body, also has a compression fitting into which you can insert tubing.

TOP: A simple way to convert to drip is to screw multioutlet emitters onto the risers. Various emitter designs are shown here—purchase a style having the number of outlets you need. For maximum flexibility, choose types that can adjust the flow via either changeable inserts or adjustable valves.

ABOVE: Another simple retrofit consists of capping all but one riser and then attaching drip components to that riser. Shown here are a threaded elbow, nipple, in-line filter, pressure regulator, and compression adapter.

RIGHT: For a larger system, start the conversion at the valve by removing a section of pipe to fit in a filter and pressure regulator. In this case, an expandable coupling reconnects the pressure regulator to the pipe. At the risers, screw on tees or elbows with compression adapters cemented into the outlets.

CONVERTING AT THE VALVE

This retrofit is suitable for larger gardens requiring more distribution lines and watering devices. It's also useful if the sprinklers are separated by paving, or if the line serves a large number of plants.

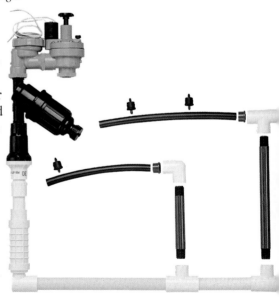

Remove the section of pipe after the valve and screw on a filter and pressure regulator. Reconnect the pipe with a coupling or other device designed to link the parts.

Screw elbows or tees onto the risers and glue on compression adapters that will accept tubing. Some sprinkler manufacturers make microspray heads that can be substituted for some models of conventional sprinkler heads; consult your irrigation supplier for these.

TIMERS

A timer, or controller, is an indispensable tool for efficient irrigation. It relieves you of having to remember when to water which plantings and how long to let the water run in each case. All but the most basic timers allow you to schedule irrigation cycles that will occur automatically at preset hours, whether in the middle of the night or while you're away on vacation. You can even direct a timer to override your instructions whenever it rains.

A dial at the hose end allows you to set the watering time on this portable sprinkler.

TYPES OF TIMERS

Irrigation suppliers, hardware stores, and home-improvement centers offer a variety of timers ranging from simple types that will shut off the flow at a single faucet to versatile controllers capable of operating a dozen or more circuits.

SIMPLE MECHANICAL TIMERS

These basic timers automate water shutoff, but because they have no power source or memory, you must set them every time you want to water. Most types attach directly to a hose bibb or to a hose-Y; some are incorporated into portable sprinklers.

You turn the dial—calibrated in minutes (and sometimes hours) or gallons, depending on the model—to the desired setting. The timer turns off automatically after the set time has expired or the set number of gallons has been dispensed. The timer usually has an override setting so you can use the faucet normally.

BATTERY-OPERATED TIMERS

Electronic circuitry makes this kind of hose bibb timer more flexible than a mechanical one—and you don't have to be there to turn on the timer each time, as you do with the simpler ones. Depending on the model, you may be able to schedule the water to turn on and off at appointed times every day, at intervals (such as every third or seventh day), or on certain days of the week. The timer will control just the one circuit hooked to the hose bibb.

Some models have a digital readout and key pads for punching in your program. Others have little dials that you turn to the desired settings. Still others provide a range of possible watering schedules keyed to numbers—you turn a dial to the desired number. An indicator that lets you know when to change the batteries is a desirable feature, because the timer's memory will fail when the batteries do.

ELECTRIC TIMERS

These timers allow you to program watering schedules for multiple irrigation circuits. You can buy an older-style electromechanical model, a newer electronic one, or an in-between type that manufacturers call a hybrid. You connect the timer to the control valves with low-voltage wire and then plug the timer's low-voltage transformer into an ordinary household electrical outlet.

TOP: This simple mechanical timer will turn the water off automatically, but it must be reset each time you want to water.

BOTTOM: A battery-operated timer will turn the water on and off according to your preset instructions.

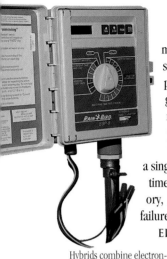

Hybrids combine electronics and mechanical dials.

ELECTROMECHANICAL. Less commonly available today than in the past, this sort of timer has gears that trip scheduling pins, switches, or levers. Though easy to program, it's not as accurate as an electronic model in controlling watering duration. Its programming capabilities are more limited, too—residential models typically have only a single program (see the descriptions of potential timer features at right). Because it has no memory, it doesn't lose its programming in a power failure; you just reset the clock.

ELECTRONIC. These computerized timers have a digital readout and keypads for inputting program instructions. There are no dials, gears, or other moving parts. Most models for home use offer two independent programs, some three. This kind of timer is very accurate, but its memory can be wiped out in a power failure—a good reason to get a model with a battery backup that will retain the programming for at least several hours.

HYBRID. This type of electric timer combines computerized circuitry and mechanical dials. When electronic controllers were first introduced, most were so difficult to program that manufacturers responded to consumer frustration with this new category of user-friendly hybrids. The timers are capable of all the functions of strictly electronic models.

HYDRAULIC TIMERS

Water-powered controllers are used in areas with frequent lightning storms, because the electrical activity interferes with the operation of electric timers. Rather than an electric remote-control valve, each irrigation circuit has a hydraulic one. A separate water-filled tube connects each valve with the designated station on the controller. Where temperatures fall below freezing in winter, the tubes must be drained and blown out with compressed air before cold weather arrives.

CHOOSING A TIMER

Before you shop, think about what you want your timer to do, so that you end up with one that meets your needs. Consider not only the number of valves you want it to control but also what programming capabilities you'd find useful (read on for a description of features offered by the more sophisticated timers). Remember, the more features and versatility, the more expensive the controller. Prices range from about $15 for the simplest timers to thousands of dollars for the ultra-high-tech types. Most electric timers for home use are priced from less than $100 to several hundred dollars.

Just as important as features and price is ease of programming. Some timers are mind-boggling in their complexity, others fairly simple. Ask to see the instructions before you buy—if you can't follow them, look for another, easier-to-understand timer.

NUMBER OF STATIONS. Each station on a timer operates one remote-control valve, so you'll need at least as many stations as you have valves in your system. If you intend to expand your system, choose a controller with one or two extra stations—or get an expandable model that allows you plug in extra stations. Timers are available with four, six, eight, or more stations—the greater the number, the more you'll pay.

NUMBER OF PROGRAMS. A program is a watering schedule for stations that will operate on the same days and for the same number of times each day. Some residential timers have a single program, which is adequate if you're watering plants with similar moisture needs. Others have two or even three independent programs, which is useful when circuits contain plants with dissimilar needs, such as lawn and mature trees. They allow you to set up different watering frequencies and durations for those different circuits. Because only one circuit can operate at once, circuits on the same program will run consecutively.

Look for useful features and programming ease in a timer.

MULTIPLE START TIMES. Just about all timers, including battery-operated types attached to hose bibbs, allow you to run a circuit more than once on each watering day. This feature allows you to pulse-irrigate, or water for short periods so that water can be absorbed without running off; it's also useful for giving container plants small amounts of water several times a day. Rather than buy a costlier timer with long run times (see below) to operate drip circuits for several hours, you could use a less expensive model with many start times to run for the same total of hours. The number of start times varies according to the timer, so be sure you get enough to serve your needs.

RUN TIMES. This refers to the watering duration. If at least some of your circuits are drip, you'll appreciate a controller that can be scheduled in hours, because drip delivers water slowly. Run times of 1 minute to 4 hours, for example, would allow you to water your container plants for a couple of minutes at a time and your mature trees for several hours.

WATERING CYCLES. A timer may have several scheduling options. A timer with a 7-day cycle repeats its programming every 7 days—inconvenient if you want to run some circuits only every couple of weeks. Timers with 14- or 15-day cycles offer more flexibility in that regard. However, if the 7-day cycle offers "skip day" intervals of up to 14 days, then you'll be able to water as desired. Many controllers offer "every day," "every second day," or "every third day" options as well.

PERCENT ADJUSTMENT. This feature, available on many slightly more expensive controllers with electronic circuity, lets you adjust the watering time by a certain percentage without reprogramming the timer. This makes it easy to cut back on watering time during cool spells in summer, increase moisture during prolonged heat waves, and adjust for seasonal changes.

RAIN OR MOISTURE SHUTOFF. A sensor linked to the timer will override the programming if a certain amount of rain has fallen or if the soil is sufficiently moist. A rain sensor or a rain collection pan should be mounted where it will be exposed to rain; a soil moisture sensor should be inserted into the ground at a representative spot. You could splice the detector into the common wire connecting the control valves to the timer, but that would prevent you from operating the timer manually (for example, to test a circuit) when the switch is activated. Rather, get a model with its own sensor terminal.

ELECTRICAL GROUNDING AND SURGE PROTECTION. These features protect the timer from lightning hits and power spikes.

PROGRAM SAVER. Most controllers with electronic circuitry have a battery backup that saves the program for at least several hours after a power outage. The amount of time varies according to the timer model.

INSTALLING THE TIMER

Begin by picking an easily accessible, well-lighted spot that has a standard electrical outlet within 6 feet. A garage, basement, utility room, laundry room, or toolshed (if it has power) is a common choice. Mount the timer at about chest height on a wall stud; follow the manufacturer's installation directions.

Connecting the valves to the timer will be much easier if you use color-coded irrigation wire.

WIRING THE VALVES TO THE TIMER

Low-voltage, insulated wire that's approved for direct burial (meaning it doesn't have to be placed in a conduit underground) is used to connect the valves to the timer. Color-coded, multistrand wire makes it easy to remember what connects with what—a different color for each valve joining it to a station on the timer, and another one (the pros usually choose white) for the common wire linking all of the valves to the timer. Thus, if you have four valves, you'll need five-strand wire. If system expansion is a possibility, get wire with extra strands so you won't have to rewire the whole system later.

To figure out how much wire to get, measure the distance from the farthest valve to the controller; then add a few feet. The

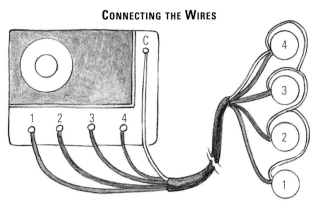

The control valve's solenoid (a sort of switch that opens and shuts the valve when signaled by the timer) has two wires sticking out of it. Connect either one of those wires on each valve to the common wire, using waterproof connectors. Attach the common wire to the common-wire screw terminal on the timer. Connect the remaining wire on each valve to the desired station on the timer. Write down which station runs which circuit and keep your notations near the timer.

most common wires for residential irrigation use are the 14- and 18-gauge sizes. Check with the manufacturer for the recommended size for your valves.

Connect the wire as shown above. Run the wire underground to the timer location. If the irrigation main is running in the same direction, take advantage of it to lay the wire in its trench, beneath the pipe for added protection. Follow the main until you are as close to the controller as possible. Leave plenty of slack as you lay the wire; the pros also loop the wire at each valve and at turns in the trench. When you get to the timer site, bring the wire above ground and tack it along walls, joists, and other surfaces as needed.

After the wiring is complete, plug in the controller and test each station manually. Program the controller according to the manufacturer's instructions. (To figure out how long and how often to water your plantings, refer to the chapter beginning on page 89.)

UPGRADING AN EXISTING SYSTEM

If you have an older irrigation system with manual valves, replacing them with remote-control types and wiring them to a timer will ease your watering chores and help you water more efficiently.

Adding a rain shutoff device is the most common upgrade for an existing automatic system. If your timer doesn't have a terminal for the device, you can get around that by connecting it to the common wire—though that will preclude manual operations when the device has turned off the system.

HOW MUCH AND HOW OFTEN?

Figuring out how much and when to water all your various plantings can be perplexing, even if you're a longtime gardener. If you water by hand, a fully automated irrigation system may seem like the answer to your problem. Such a setup will relieve you of a lot of work, but it won't run completely on its own— you must program it for duration and frequency.

So there is no way to avoid addressing the "how much" and "how often" of watering, whether your system is sophisticated or low-tech. The techniques described in this chapter will set you on the right path, though: rather than try to master complicated formulas, you can simply water to root depth and then reapply moisture when the root zone dries out. A soil probe that removes a core of soil can help you determine how long to let the water run and how soon to water again.

For selected plants (primarily lawn), scientific watering schedules based on the rate at which water is depleted from the soil are available to gardeners in some regions. But even with these timetables or ones you've devised yourself, you should still monitor your plants and check your soil so that you can make adjustments as needed.

A rain barrel filled with water stands ready to be used when plants need it.

When irrigating by hand, you may think you're applying more water than you actually are. To be sure that moisture is penetrating deep enough, check the soil in the plant's root zone.

WHAT DOES THAT MEAN?

"Water deeply but infrequently" is a common suggestion. *Deeply* is sometimes interpreted as watering many feet deep, but actually it simply means getting moisture to the roots. Thus, *deeply* is a relative term that can mean 2 feet for some plants but only 6 inches for others.

People for whom watering is a disagreeable chore may read *infrequently* as "hardly ever"—which may in fact be appropriate for very drought-tolerant plants. But a more apt interpretation is that water applied to root depth will last longer and can be reapplied less often than a mere moistening of the surface. Thus, *infrequently* can mean every few days or every few weeks, depending on the plant, the weather, the soil texture, and other factors.

WATERING STRATEGIES

When should I water? How much is enough? When should I water again?

These are among the questions that novice gardeners most often ask, usually expecting to receive simple answers. Unfortunately, straightforward, suit-any-situation responses are in short supply when it comes to irrigation, as experienced gardeners know.

Some common pointers—for example, "water when the plant needs it" or "apply as much as the plant requires for healthy growth"—are too vague to be of much help. Another familiar, imprecise recommendation is to "water deeply but infrequently" (see at left). At odds with this counsel is some people's advice to apply tiny amounts of water frequently, even daily, so that plants have continual access to moisture—reasonable advice for edibles, but not necessarily for other plants.

Exact watering prescriptions may be more satisfying than the hazy guidance cited above, but they aren't always practical. For example, conventional wisdom calls for at least 1 inch of water a week, with you, the gardener, applying whatever nature doesn't. Even if you know that 62 gallons will cover a 100-square-foot area with a 1-inch "layer" of water, you must still figure out when you've applied the magic inch, given your own particular application method. And before you begin your calculations, you should realize that an inch isn't always appropriate—any individual plant's actual need may be for more or less. Furthermore, the inch of water will penetrate deeper and last longer in some soil types than others. So even this prescription isn't as precise as it appears to be.

Although an uncomplicated watering formula would simplify every gardener's life, there just isn't one that applies to an entire garden of mixed plantings. However, lawn-watering schedules based on the local evapotranspiration (ET) rate are used in many areas, and additional schedules for selected ornamental plants are becoming available in some parts of the West; see page 94 for more information. As for the other plantings in your garden, you'll have to water them taking into account your plants' needs, the weather, your soil texture, and your method of application.

Unless you want to turn gardening into a mathematical exercise, as the developers of ET-based watering schedules have, the best general advice is to water to the depth of a plant's root zone and then apply more water when the root zone dries out. (Remember, some plants have special needs, so inquire when you obtain a plant.) The discussion that follows explains why it's important to focus on wetting the soil where the roots are growing, and details easy ways to accomplish that task.

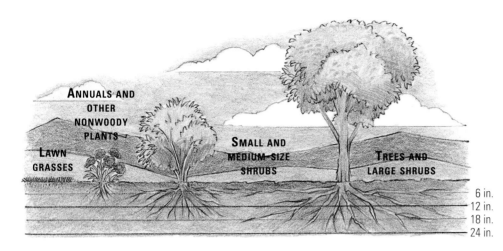

When following the advice to water to a plant's root depth, you'll accomplish your goal if you use the depth guidelines illustrated at left. Note that most of the feeder roots of even large trees are within the top 2 feet of soil, and that they extend well beyond the plant's leafy top. However, because they are still deeper than grass roots, don't assume lawn irrigation will supply the needs of trees growing in turf.

6 in.
12 in.
18 in.
24 in.

WATERING TO ROOT DEPTH

We've already seen (pages 24–25) just how essential water is to plant life. A plant's root hairs are the conduits through which it absorbs moisture and requisite minerals, which can be taken up only when dissolved in water. Thus, getting moisture to the level of the root hairs is vital, but watering any deeper is wasteful.

There's no need to water seedlings and small transplants any deeper than a few inches. But once a plant's roots have established and begun to grow into the soil, you should water to the full depth that they'll grow when given adequate moisture. But how deep is that? Roots will grow a little deeper in a loose, porous soil than in a heavy, tight one, but generally figure on growth to the following depths: lawn grasses, within the top 4 to 6 inches; annuals and other herbaceous (nonwoody) plants, within the top 12 inches; small and medium-size shrubs, within the top 12 to 18 inches; and trees and large shrubs, within the top 24 inches. Though you might think you'd have to water large trees much deeper, in fact most of their feeder roots are located within the top couple of feet; the deeper roots mainly anchor the tree.

Watering to the recommended depth encourages roots to grow there, just as shallow watering keeps roots near the soil surface. Deeper roots have access to more moisture and can go longer between waterings; they're also less subject to stress from heat and drying winds than shallow roots are.

When you're watering trees and shrubs, depth is only part of the story. You should also keep in mind the width of the root zone—in mature plants, it may extend from one-and-a-half (in clay soils) to three times (in sandy soils) the diameter of the plant's foliage or crown.

CONSIDERING SOIL

You must apply enough water to percolate down into the soil and wet the plant's root zone. This is where soil texture comes into play. Water enters loose, sandy soils and porous potting mixes faster than it does loam or tight clay soils. Also, the same amount of water moves downward more quickly and penetrates to a greater depth in loose soils than in denser soils (see the illustra-

tion on page 27). That's because water tends to go straight down in the looser types but spreads more laterally in the tighter ones. As a result, you must water a clay soil longer than a sandy one to get water to root depth; on the plus side, the clay soil will retain moisture longer.

A soil's infiltration rate—the amount of water in inches that can enter the soil in an hour—affects how long you can irrigate before the water starts to run off. The following are the average rates at which water can enter various soil types. Note that the intake rate decreases over time—it may be greater than the rate indicated during the first 10 minutes or so, and then slow to less than what's shown here.

- Sandy soils   ¾ to 1½ inches per hour
- Loam   ¼ to ¾ inch per hour
- Clay soils   ¹⁄₁₀ to ¼ inch per hour

PREVENTING RUNOFF. You don't usually have to worry about runoff when you're applying small amounts of water slowly—for example, with drip emitters or microsprays. But if you're using conventional underground or portable sprinklers, which dispense up to several gallons per minute (gpm), you must take care not to run your system past the point at which the soil can absorb the moisture. The type of sprinkler affects when you reach that point: a rotary head (rotor), for instance, that applies 6 or 7 gpm will cause less runoff than a spray head dispensing 3 or 4 gpm. That's because the rotor has a lower precipitation rate (the amount of water applied in inches per hour), given that it covers a larger area and makes less frequent passes over each section.

Rotors like this gear-driven model have a lower precipitation rate than spray heads do.

FORMING INDIVIDUAL BASINS
Build up the soil on the downhill side of the tree, so that water running down the slope will pool inside the basin and soak in.

TERRACING
This technique allows you to level out the soil over the root zone, so that water can seep in instead of running off. Install header boards across the slope at the outside edge of the root zone; then add soil to within a couple of inches of the top of the board.

To determine the precipitation rate of your sprinkler system, conduct a catch-can test (see page 95). If your system puts out 1 inch of water per hour but your soil type can absorb only ¼ inch per hour, you can run the sprinklers for only 15 minutes at a time before water begins to run off.

Even simpler than calculating your precipitation rate is turning on your sprinklers and noting how long it takes for runoff to occur—you then operate your system just short of that in the future. If water doesn't penetrate to root depth in the allotted time, you can pulse-irrigate: water in short cycles, with rest periods between cycles to allow the moisture to soak in. An automatic timer with several start times will simplify this process.

Another way to avoid runoff is to slow down the delivery rate. If your sprinklers put out a lot of water quickly, you can switch to types with a lower precipitation rate. As a group, rotors apply less water over a given area than spray heads do; among spray heads, those sold as low-precipitation-rate models apply the least water. Switching to a drip system, of course, will drastically retard the rate at which water is applied.

When hand-watering, you can control the application rate by turning the faucet on low. Keep water from running off by directing it into basins or furrows you've formed around plants, or by using a deep-root irrigator.

If your soil is compacted or crusted over, even small amounts of irrigation water or light rainfall may be unable to infiltrate it, and water in basins or furrows will be slow to soak in. To improve the soil's ability to accept moisture, work in lots of organic matter and top the amended soil with a layer of mulch. Slowly applied water that runs off a lawn indicates the need to aerate and dethatch (see page 20).

Note how long it takes water to run off; then run your sprinkler a bit less than that the next time.

HOW MUCH?

So you know that it's important to get water to the plant's root zone, but how much water does that translate into? You can apply a certain number of gallons or inches of water if you know the plant's exact need—for example, when following an ET-based lawn-watering schedule. In most cases, though, it's easier to approach watering from the point of view of how long you let the water run, rather than what specific amount of water you apply.

As we've seen, a plant's root depth and the type of soil in which it grows are factors in how long you water it. Just as important is your application method, because different methods apply water at different rates. If you water with sprinkler spray heads, you'll get the job done faster than you will with rotors. If you water with a drip system or soaker hoses, you'll need to schedule a lot more time.

Because it takes longer for water to reach deeper roots, you must water deeper-rooted plants longer than shallower types—assuming that you're using the same watering method.

The simplest way to figure out how long to water a specific planting is to apply water and note how long it takes for a barely dry root zone to become wet; you then run your system for that length of time in the future. To ascertain how deeply the water has penetrated, you could dig down with a trowel or shovel, but that's a lot of work and can damage the planting. Soil probes and moisture meters offer quicker, easier ways to find out what's happening underground.

SOIL PROBES

Technically, any long metal rod—even a long screwdriver—pushed into the ground can serve as a soil probe. Such a rod will move easily through moist soil but slow down noticeably or stop when it reaches dry soil, allowing you to estimate the depth of moisture.

However, a probe that extracts a core of soil (sometimes called a soil sampling tube or soil corer) actually shows you the level of moisture below ground. As shown at left, it consists of a hollow metal tube, slotted down one side, with a bar across the top for pushing it into the earth and pulling it back out with a core of soil. An 18-inch-long soil probe is sufficient for most plantings; one model has holes at 2-inch intervals that enable you to quickly gauge moisture penetration and root depth. A more expensive 3-foot-long probe is also sold. (See page 111 for some soil probe vendors.)

To find out if you've watered to root depth, use the soil probe after irrigating. Adjust the watering time based on what you see—for example, if the core is moist only 2 inches deep, yet those plants' roots could easily go down 6 inches, you need to water about three times as long. Irrigate again and take another sample. After you've used the probe to check water penetration several times in a planting, you'll know how long it takes for your irrigation system to wet your soil to the depth you want, and you can water accordingly—with seasonal adjustments, of course.

SOIL MOISTURE METERS

Moisture meters sold for home use typically have a probe attached to a dial or scale that shows relative wetness or dryness. The kind designed for houseplants will stand up to use in potting soils, but the probe is usually too short and

This lightweight meter is suitable only for measuring moisture a few inches deep, in porous soil mixes.

flimsy to be of much use in gauging the moisture level of in-ground outdoor plantings.

Outdoor models tend to be pricey and hard to find. One battery-operated model has a 2-foot-long probe and a readout that assesses moisture on a scale from 0 (dry) to 10 (wet).

HOW OFTEN?

Once you are watering to the proper depth, the next question is, How do you tell when it's time to water again? Your natural inclination may be to water when the soil surface is dry, but you should be concerned instead with the moisture level in the root zone.

A soil probe that extracts a core of soil will help you decide when to reapply water. If the soil sample is dry on top but moist where the roots are growing, hold off on watering. A lack of adequate moisture in the root zone signals that it's time to water. For many

A rain gauge will tell you how much rain has fallen.

plants, this means soil that is "barely" dry—not bone dry or powder dry—throughout the core. For moisture-loving plants, water again when the soil is still a bit moist at root level. After a while, you'll have a good sense of when you need to irrigate without checking the soil each time.

If you want to stretch watering intervals to their limit, you can observe your plants to see how long it takes them to show signs of water stress (see below). The next time, don't wait quite so long. You'll soon get a feel for how long your plants can go between irrigations without suffering any ill effects. (Don't do this with edibles, especially vegetables, though; they'll be more succulent and flavorful if given a steady supply of moisture.)

The interval between irrigations depends on how fast the water in the soil has been depleted by the plants (some use more moisture than others) and by other factors, including temperature, wind, humidity, and day length. Whether it has rained since you last watered is clearly another key element. If these circumstances

---

OBSERVE YOUR PLANTS

Your plants will show visible signs when the soil's too dry. Shiny leaves lose their luster, normally bright green foliage may take on a blue or gray cast, leaf edges curl, and growth slows; eventually, the plants wilt. In hot weather, insufficiently watered plants may develop scorched leaves—it begins as yellowing and browning along the leaf edges and may extend in toward the veins. Water stress can

cause plants to lose leaves, vegetables to turn bitter, tomatoes to develop blossom-end rot, and fruit trees to drop fruit.

By observing your plants, you can learn to recognize the signs of water stress and irrigate before the damage becomes irreversible.

Evenly moist soil prevents blossom-end rot in tomatoes.

This large, fence-mounted rain gauge can be read at a glance.

ET ON THE INTERNET

Computer-savvy gardeners can consult the World Wide Web for some help in figuring out how often they should water. One site—www.wateright.org—provides Californians with irrigation schedules for lawns as well as selected ornamental plants. Plans are under way to expand the program to more states, starting with western ones.

The website's program asks you to enter a variety of information: specifics about your underground sprinkler or drip system, plant type, closest weather station (from a list supplied), and the number of waterings you want per week. Based on those data, the program will produce a yearlong watering schedule that can be updated regularly.

The developers of this website caution that the schedules are not intended to replace your own observation of your plants or soil. Rather, they serve as a starting point that you can adjust to meet your specific needs.

never varied, you could water your garden by the calendar. However, you'd be under- or overwatering your plants at times if you reapplied moisture at set periods, disregarding the weather or season.

You must water more often during very hot, dry, or windy weather. When it's cool or humid, less frequent watering is in order. In winter, when the days are short and the sun is low on the horizon (diminishing light intensity and thereby lowering plant water use), even nondormant plants demand much less water than they do in summer.

Always take rain into account, because it potentially frees you from the task of watering, at least for a while. But don't assume that rain is fulfilling your plants' needs—it may just be wetting the soil surface and cleansing the foliage. For a more accurate picture of what's fallen, keep a rain gauge handy and check how much water has collected. (Be aware that although a thunderstorm may dump a lot of water on your garden, it won't do your plants much good if most of it runs off.)

Your Cooperative Extension office, water company, or local nurseries may advise watering some plantings at set intervals based on local weather conditions. These schedules may be fine as guides, but you'd be wise to check your soil to see what's happening in *your* garden.

Remember, your own schedule is also just a starting point—be prepared to make adjustments to reflect changes in the weather and the passage of seasons. For an automated system, a timer with a percent adjustment feature (see page 87) makes this easy. And if you're starting from scratch with a new landscape, you'll have to make changes as the plants mature.

WHAT'S THE BEST TIME OF DAY?

To minimize water loss from evaporation, especially if you're running sprinklers, water early in the morning, before the sun is most intense and while the air is relatively calm. Watering then will also give the foliage of moisture-sensitive plants plenty of time to dry, reducing their chances of developing leaf diseases. A bonus is that your water pressure will be higher during the early hours.

Between 3:00 and 6:00 A.M. is considered ideal—but of course, such early irrigation is practical only for automated systems. Be sure to set the timer so that the irrigation cycles are all completed before your indoor household water use begins for the day.

The time of day matters less when you irrigate with drip emitters and soaker hoses, because there is little or no water loss to evaporation. Even if your water pressure is at an ebb period, it doesn't matter, because those systems work best at lower pressures.

WATERING BY ET

An irrigation schedule based on the local evapotranspiration (ET) rate—the amount of water that evaporates from the soil plus the amount that transpires through the plants' leaves—offers a precise way to water. The idea is that if you know the rate of water depletion (expressed in inches), you know exactly how much to reapply.

The ET rate is variable, because it depends on the plant species as well as on weather conditions—including temperature, humidity, wind speed, and cloud cover. It also varies by locality, though in all parts of North America it is lowest in winter, increasing in spring, peaking in summer, and decreasing in autumn.

ET-based irrigation was developed for commercial growers raising a single type of uniformly spaced crop; thus, it isn't easily applied to the mixed, irregularly spaced plantings found in home gardens. An exception is lawn—because of its uniformity, it lends itself very well to an ET-based schedule.

SEASONAL WATER USE

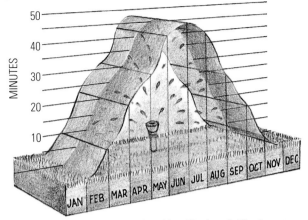

This irrigation schedule was developed by a Northern California water district to illustrate the maximum weekly water needs of lawns in its service area. The weekly sprinkler run time (the "minutes" column) is based on an application rate of 2 inches per hour.

Because turf accounts for the bulk of outdoor water use in arid and semiarid regions, many Cooperative Extension offices and water companies in those areas provide homeowners with ET information for watering their lawns. To find out if there's a local schedule for your area, contact either entity. In some areas, the Internet is another source of ET guides for lawn as well as certain other ornamentals; see the facing page. To follow any of these schedules, you must know your sprinkler output in inches; a catch-can test will give you the answer (see at right).

ET lawn-watering schedules are based on averages; they don't take your specific grass mix and soil conditions into account. Use the chart figure as a starting point; then observe your lawn for a few weeks, using a soil probe to see for yourself what's happening at root level. If the soil in the root zone is drying out before the next scheduled irrigation, water for slightly longer periods or for shorter, more frequent periods. If water is penetrating below the root zone, cut back on the volume or the frequency of irrigation until the lawn begins to dry out between waterings; then add a few minutes to get back on track.

Commercial growers obtain up-to-the-minute ET figures, so they can alter their watering schedules to reflect changing conditions. Most lawn-watering charts prepared for homeowners simply list by month the amount of water recommended for each irrigation. A certain frequency is advised—for example, every 2 days or every 3 days. Because these are set figures based on average weather conditions in previous years, you must make your own alterations as needed. On exceptionally hot, clear, dry, windy days, for instance, you may have to apply more water than what's listed on the chart. Unseasonably cool weather or prolonged cloudiness may let you postpone watering for several days. Again, a soil probe will help you determine whether the root zone is adequately moist.

CATCH-CAN TEST

Here's a simple test to find out how much water your sprinklers—either portable or underground—are spraying, measured in inches per hour. You may want to know this in order to follow an ET-based lawn-watering schedule, or to determine whether your spray coverage is uniform.

Place several containers of the same size and shape throughout the lawn or other planting area—though the photo below shows a regular pattern, the containers can be positioned randomly. The containers can be square or round but should have a flat bottom and straight sides (a minor slant to the sides will slightly overestimate the amount of water being applied, but that shouldn't be a problem). Coffee mugs are a good choice. Don't use very short containers like small tuna cans, because water will splash out; also avoid containers taller than about 6 inches, because some water will hit the outer walls instead of landing inside.

Run your underground sprinklers or portable sprinkler for 15 minutes (or for some other period that divides evenly into 60 minutes). With a ruler, measure the depth of the water in each container, add the figures together, and divide by the number of containers to determine the average amount of water. Multiply by 4 (or by 6 if you ran the water for 10 minutes, by 3 if you ran it for 20 minutes) to determine the output of your sprinkler system in inches per hour. For example, if the average amount applied in 15 minutes is ⅜ inch, the hourly rate is 1½ inches. If there is more than a ¼-inch difference among containers, check your sprinkler heads to see if they need adjusting or reposition your portable sprinkler; then run the test again.

A catch-can test will reveal how much water your portable or underground sprinklers are applying—and whether the distribution is uniform.

WATERING YOUR
PLANTS

When nature takes over the job of watering your garden, you don't usually worry about how it's done—unless the rain arrives in torrents and batters or washes away plants. When you're responsible for supplying moisture, however, technique comes into play. Will you water by hand, flood a soil basin, rely on soaker hoses, apply water in drips, or imitate nature and sprinkle?

The answer depends on the type of plantings you have as well as on your climate, soil, garden size, and budget. Some irrigation methods are better suited to certain plantings—for example, you wouldn't use a watering can to irrigate a lawn, but you might use it for a few potted plants. If your container collection grew, hand watering could become tedious, so you might choose an automated drip system. You'd be more likely to invest in a permanent drip or sprinkler system for much of your landscape in a dry-summer climate than in one where irrigation is an occasional activity.

In this chapter you'll find watering guidelines for some of the most common types of plantings. Keep in mind that some plants within a category may need special watering. For details about delivery systems—garden hoses, soaker hoses, portable sprinklers, underground sprinklers, and drip networks—see the chapter beginning on page 45.

Overhead watering of tall plants like foxgloves can cause them to tip over.

In summer-rainfall climates, portable sprinklers are the usual way to water lawns when nature fails to provide the necessary moisture.

LAWNS

During warm weather most lawns demand lots of water—it's often said between 1 and 2 inches a week—for healthy, attractive growth. If you garden in a dry-summer climate, you must supply the necessary moisture. If you're in a summer-rainfall area, you'll only have to irrigate when rain doesn't come abundantly enough or at the right time.

SIGNS OF THIRST

You'll know your grass needs water if you walk across the lawn and your footprints remain visible for more than a few seconds. Another sign of thirst is a dull appearance, caused by the grass blades folding up and exposing their bases.

Most people apply even more water than their turf needs, thus promoting fast growth and frequent mowing, and sometimes causing the grass to become diseased. Like other plants, turf grasses need moisture at the root zone. The roots of most conventional lawns are fairly shallow—usually 4 to 6 inches deep—so water applied much deeper is wasted. The lawn should not be watered again until the root zone dries out. If you're not sure whether you're watering to the correct depth or whether the roots are drying out, check with a soil probe (see page 93).

When it does rain, you can't always assume that nature has watered your lawn adequately. A rain gauge will suggest whether enough rain has fallen during the week. But if what seems like sufficient rain came in a short, intense storm, much of it probably ran off. Again, checking moisture at the root zone with a soil probe will tell you whether you actually need to irrigate.

As a water conservation measure, many water districts and Cooperative Extension offices in drier regions have developed lawn watering schedules for homeowners based on the local evapotranspiration (ET) rate—the amount of water that evaporates from the soil plus the amount that transpires through the blades of grass. If you know what that rate is, you can apply an equal amount of water to replace the lost moisture. See page 94 for more about watering based on ET.

If, during normal irrigation or a fairly light rain, water runs off before it can soak in, check to see if your lawn has a thatch buildup that is repelling water or if the soil has become compacted. (See page 20 for information on dethatching and aerating.) Also, when you're watering with sprinklers, try "pulsing" your irrigation—divide the total watering period into several shorter intervals to allow time for the water to soak in.

WATERING METHODS

The usual way to irrigate lawns is with sprinklers, either portable types or a permanent underground system of spray heads or rotary heads (rotors). Drip irrigation for lawns is only a recent development.

All methods can be automated, but you must be careful not to program the waterings and forget about them. Be ready to make alterations when the weather changes. A soil probe will also help you fine-tune your original schedule.

PORTABLE SPRINKLERS. These hose-end attachments, which offer the simplest, least expensive way to water a lawn, are relied on mainly in areas where irrigation is a backup to the primary source of moisture: rain. Choose a sprinkler with a pattern that most closely matches the size and shape of your lawn.

To avoid having to move a sprinkler around for good coverage, you may want to operate more than one—simultaneously or consecutively, depending on your water capacity. You can connect each sprinkler to a separate faucet or to the branches of a Y attachment on one faucet.

Because portable sprinklers vary greatly in the amount of water dispensed, run the sprinkler to see how long it takes to wet the lawn's root zone; operate it for that amount of time thereafter.

ANOTHER OPTION

Wick irrigation systems, which dispense water frugally by capillary (wicking) action, are available in some areas—but they're not intended for installation by do-it-yourselfers. They go together the way conventional PVC sprinkler systems do, operating at similar pressure levels for similar run times, but they don't waste water by overspraying.

UNDERGROUND SPRINKLER SYSTEMS. In regions where lawn irrigation is a regular task, you may want to invest in a traditional underground sprinkler system. A well-designed setup will water more accurately than a portable sprinkler, with less waste. Polyvinyl chloride (PVC) or polyethylene pipes connect a series of pop-up heads, carefully spaced for complete lawn coverage. See pages 55–67 for specifics on designing and installing such a system.

A simpler version, featuring special polyethylene hoses and self-draining heads, is available in kit form. It is beneficial mainly in freezing climates, because the hose doesn't have to be buried below the frost line and doesn't have to be blown out before cold weather arrives. See page 55 for details.

Underground sprinklers
ease the job of watering.

UNDERGROUND DRIP SYSTEMS. The same type of emitter line used on the soil surface has recently been adapted for use underground, to water lawns. The emitters are generally clog resistant, though one manufacturer has treated its emitters with an herbicide to keep grass roots out.

Underground drip is not recommended for very porous or gravelly soils, those infested with gophers or other burrowing animals, or those containing a lot of tree roots. It's best used in places where sprinklers don't work well: narrow strips, very irregular shapes, steep slopes, and mounds.

The system can be installed in an existing lawn by trenching down or inserting the tubing with a vibratory plow, just as you would install underground sprinklers in existing turf. In this case, the lawn can be drip watered right after installation. With new lawns, you'll have to water the surface by hand or with a portable sprinkler for a little while. Keep new sod watered for the first couple of weeks; seeded lawns, until the roots are well established.

Learning how often to run an underground drip system requires some experimentation. Be careful when using a soil probe to check moisture levels—dig down carefully with a trowel to locate test areas in between emitter lines, and note their location so you can sink a probe without damaging the tubing.

See page 81 for details on installing a system; however, unless you have lots of experience with drip irrigation, you may want to leave the job to a professional.

Water trickling from preinstalled underground drip emitters spreads slowly through the soil to irrigate the grass.

VEGETABLES

Giving vegetables the water they need is especially critical, because you'll be eating them. With adequate water, vegetables develop crispness and flavor; without it, they become bitter and tough or dried out.

You'll be able to water more efficiently if you plant your vegetables according to their water needs. Group them by how big they get and how fast they grow; the bigger and faster growing they are, the more water they'll use. Shallow-rooted plants like beets, bush beans, carrots, lettuce, spinach and other greens, and radishes grow at about the same rate and use similar amounts of water—though leafy vegetables will need a little more water than root crops. Corn, cucumber, melons, tomatoes, and squash combine well, too, as they all grow rapidly and need ample moisture.

Don't mix new plantings of a particular crop with existing ones, because seedlings and mature plants have different irrigation needs. Larger plants need more water, to a greater depth. Young ones, with their small, shallow roots, must be watered more frequently—as often as two or three times a day—to keep them moist.

Squash plants often droop on warm days, but they should revive if given regular moisture. Furrows are a good way to get water to the roots of squash and other plants that don't appreciate wet leaves. Limit your furrows to about 12 feet long in clay soil, about half that length in sandy soil.

WATERING METHODS

In summer-rainfall climates, gardeners can usually get away with hand watering and using portable sprinklers and soaker hoses to supplement the rain. In dry-summer climates, investing in a drip system makes good sense. In arid areas that get some rain in summer, such as parts of the Southwest, try forming basins and furrows—or even sunken beds (see page 42)—to catch water and channel it to plant roots.

HAND WATERING. If you have a very small garden or live in a rainy climate, you may not want anything more complicated than a watering can or a garden hose. The watering can will also be handy for applying liquid fertilizer. Be sure to use a hose-end nozzle with an especially gentle spray, or a watering can with a "rose" (a wide, perforated head at the end of the spout), when watering seedbeds and young transplants.

Getting water to the roots of large plants can take longer than you think when you're hand-watering. Here's a trick to deliver water quickly to the root zone: partially bury a large juice can, an upside-down plastic milk jug with the bottom cut off, or a short length of large-diameter PVC pipe next to the plant; place the hose end into the conduit and slowly run the water.

Connecting several basins streamlines the job of watering—set the garden hose down and let it fill the extended hollow while you attend to some other chore.

BASINS AND FURROWS. Form watering basins around individual large plants such as tomatoes and peppers by mounding soil about 3 inches high all the way around each one. Fill the basin with water and let it soak in—use a soil probe to see how many times you have to fill the basin to get water to root depth. On level ground, you can link several basins, as shown above.

Furrows are ditches, 3 to 8 inches deep, formed alongside crops grown in straight rows on level ground in not-too-sandy soil; see at left. When forming a long furrow, slope it slightly and fill it from the higher end. As with watering basins, use a soil probe to determine whether you must fill the furrow more than once to moisten the soil to root depth.

DRIP IRRIGATION. Rather than watering only when the root zone dries out, some experts advise applying tiny amounts of

CRITICAL WATERING PERIODS

Many vegetables need more water at certain stages of development than at others. Here are the critical periods for some widely grown vegetable crops.

Beans, peas	Flowering, pod filling
Broccoli, cabbage, cauliflower	Head development
Carrots, beets	Seed emergence, root development
Corn	Silking, tasseling, ear development
Cucumbers, melons	Flowering, fruit development
Onions	Bulb enlargement
Tomatoes, peppers, eggplant	Flowering, fruiting

Blue Lake beans

water daily, to ensure that the plants never lack moisture. Drip irrigation allows you to do this. The various delivery options include emitter line, drip tape, individual drip emitters, and microsprays.

Emitter line is especially well suited to vegetables planted in intensive beds or rows. It will fit any bed shape, water evenly on slopes, and wet the entire bed—plus you can easily lift out the tubing with its incorporated emitters whenever you want to amend the bed and replant. You'll get the best results with emitters closely spaced, just a foot apart. In sandy loams and clay soils, ½-gallon-per-hour (gph) emitters will moisten the whole planting; to get a more horizontal spread of moisture in very sandy soils, you can use 1- or even 2-gph emitters. Plant larger vegetables like corn singly on each side of the emitter line, but double up smaller plants like carrots and radishes on either side.

Drip tape is a less expensive, shorter-lived option than emitter line. Used mainly in agriculture, drip tape will water crops grown in straight rows on fairly flat terrain, much as flooded furrows do. The tape comes in several weights—the heavier types last longer.

For vegetables spaced far apart or scattered here and there, use individual drip emitters inserted directly into ⅜- or ½-inch solid drip hose, or at the end of microtubing connected to the drip hose. Position the emitters at the base of individual plants.

Microsprays are useful for crops that benefit from a moist, humid environment, such as lettuce grown from seed in a hot climate. (You're better off using another method that doesn't wet the leaves of moisture-sensitive plants like cucumbers, melons, squash, and potatoes, however.) The little sprayers are also practical for crops growing in very sandy soils, where lateral movement of water dispensed in drips is severely restricted.

See pages 68–84 for more on drip systems.

SOAKER HOSES. You can snake soaker hoses around plants or lay them along rows of vegetables. A soaker hose can't water as many plants as a true drip circuit, and it won't water evenly on slopes, but it's fairly inexpensive and simple to set up.

Of the various types sold, a flat perforated hose becomes a soaker when laid with the holes facing down; with the holes facing up, it acts as a sprinkler. Another type will ooze water when operated at low pressure. Ideally it should be connected to a pressure regulator, just as a drip irrigation circuit is, though you can turn the faucet on low or place a washer in the connection to limit the pressure. Use a filter to help keep the hose from clogging.

PORTABLE SPRINKLERS. Hose-end sprinklers are often used in vegetable beds as a backup to rainfall. As with microsprays (see "Drip Irrigation," above), it's best not to use them on disease-prone plants, especially in humid climates.

WILTING MAY MISLEAD

A wilting plant will usually send you scurrying for the watering can or garden hose, but some vegetables may wilt even with adequate moisture. Tomatoes, peppers, eggplant, and squash often droop slightly during warm days but recover at night. Check the soil before assuming the plants need more water.

Emitter line—consisting of drip tubing with preinstalled emitters spaced at regular intervals—will moisten an entire vegetable bed. Unlike a soaker hose, it is clog resistant and can be used on slopes.

Flower Beds

A flower bed may consist solely of annuals, perennials, or bulbs—or be a mixture. In a mixed planting, note that the different plant types may have somewhat different watering needs.

Annuals are short-lived plants that grow, bloom, produce seeds, and die—all within the same year. If they are to put on a good show they must grow continuously, without slowing down. That means no letup in moisture until flowering is finished.

Perennials are longer-lived plants that need regular moisture from the onset of growth until they finish blooming, just as annuals do. Unlike annuals, however, they build up reserves of nutrients for the next year before entering dormancy—which may consist of ceasing growth, losing leaves, or dying to the ground. Thus they still need some moisture from the end of bloom until dormancy; after that some perennials tolerate routine watering, whereas others prefer or actually require drier conditions.

Bulbs and bulblike plants—those growing from an underground food storage structure—need moisture from the start of growth until some point after blooming. Deciduous bulbs typically enter dormancy a month or so after flowering. Some dormant bulbs can take moist conditions and others can't, so it's important to know a bulb's needs before planting it among annuals and perennials that will be watered. Evergreen bulbs have no true dormant period; they can be watered as needed throughout the year.

WATERING METHODS

You can water a flower bed by hand or with sprinklers, soaker hoses, or drip irrigation.

HAND WATERING. A smallish bed may demand nothing more than a garden hose or a watering can. A gentle-spray nozzle attachment will keep plants from being battered. Note: when hand-watering you may think you're applying more water than you really are; check the root zone to see if it's moist.

PORTABLE SPRINKLERS. A hose-end sprinkler is often the method of choice in summer-rainfall climates. Many models are available, including elevated types that are useful when positioning the sprinkler among tall plants. Because portable sprinklers

A microspray (top) gently showers plants, whereas a soaker hose (bottom) lets water ooze into the ground.

vary in the amount of water dispensed, run yours and note how long it takes to moisten the soil to root depth (use a soil probe to determine this).

SPRINKLING ALERT

Some flowers, like zinnias and petunias, are more prone to disease when kept constantly moist, so any sprinkling or overhead hand watering that wets flowers should be done early in the day, allowing them to dry by nightfall. Other disadvantages of overhead watering are that it may cause taller plants to tip over and that it can "wash" the color from some flowers.

UNDERGROUND SPRINKLER SYSTEMS. In drier regions, a lawn sprinkler system is often extended to flower beds. The flowers are often irrigated with stationary heads rather than pop-ups (the risers should be tall enough so the spray isn't blocked by foliage) and are watered on a different circuit than the lawn. See pages 55–67 for more information.

SOAKER HOSES. Snake a soaker hose through a bed or lay it along a row of plants. Place the flat perforated kind with its holes down (upward-facing holes will spurt water). The oozing type will water most evenly on level terrain and at low pressure—use a pressure regulator (and a filter to keep the pores from clogging), insert a washer in the connection, or turn the water on low.

DRIP IRRIGATION. Using an emitter line is an easy way to water a bed of closely spaced plants; individual drip emitters are a better option for individual large or widely spaced plants. Drip applies water more precisely than spray does, and it keeps the aboveground plant parts dry. Microsprays can easily cover a large planting, applying water more slowly than standard sprinklers; overspray and blocked spray tend to be problems, however. See pages 68–84 for more on drip systems.

GROUND COVERS

Ground covers—basically, any low-growing, dense plants that blanket the ground and bind the soil—include various perennials, shrubs, and vines. Often used as alternatives to high-maintenance turf, they are less demanding of water because their roots sink deeper than those of lawn grasses. Though these plants share an ability to carpet the ground, they are otherwise diverse in appearance as well as growing requirements.

How the plant grows determines whether you treat it individually or as a mass planting, like a lawn. Some ground covers send out horizontal branches—they are individual plants, but give the impression of a uniform planting when closely spaced. This type of ground cover can be watered as if the plants were separate, because each has its own root system. Other ground covers spread by underground runners or branches that root, so it's difficult to identify separate plants. It's better to water these plants as a mass.

WATERING METHODS

The two main methods for watering a ground cover are sprinklers (either portable or underground) and drip irrigation.

PORTABLE SPRINKLERS. Where rain provides much of the moisture, a hose-end sprinkler is an easy backup tool. Moving the sprinkler around to get good coverage can be tedious, so

select a model whose spray pattern most closely conforms to the size and shape of your planting. To get the spray over the top of a tall ground cover, you can place it on a platform (such as a heavy, overturned pot) or buy an elevated sprinkler.

Portable sprinklers vary in water output. Let your sprinkler run long enough to wet the plants' root zone (use a soil probe to monitor this), note the amount of time it took, and run it that long in the future.

UNDERGROUND SPRINKLER SYSTEMS. In drier regions, the more expensive option of automated sprinklers makes sense. The height limit on pop-up heads is about a foot, so for taller plantings choose stationary heads (spray types for smaller areas and rotors for larger ones). Be sure the risers elevate the heads above the foliage—you'll have to account for the mature height of the ground cover at the time of installation. Choose low-precipitation heads for watering ground covers on slopes. For more details on sprinkler systems, see pages 55–67.

DRIP IRRIGATION. Drip emitters are suitable for individual plants such as shrubby ground covers. Water placement is more precise than with other options, and the emitters can be completely hidden from view.

Microsprays are better for closely spaced perennial ground covers and those that root along spreading stems. You can also use them to water shrubby ground covers. Because minisprays (available in various patterns) disperse water short distances, they are preferable to conventional sprinklers in narrow or tight plantings. Minisprinklers (available in full circles) spray larger areas, up to about 30 feet in diameter.

For information on putting together a drip system, see pages 68–84.

Microsprays water a planting of mixed ground covers growing on a slope. They apply water much more slowly than do conventional sprinklers, thereby lessening the likelihood of runoff.

TREES AND LARGE SHRUBS

The basin around this newly planted conifer will have to be enlarged as the plant grows.

You must get water to the root systems of these large plants, just as you do with smaller plants. You may think that you have to soak the soil many feet deep, but most feeder roots of even very large trees are within the top 2 feet of soil, so watering deeper is a waste. Though established plants are often pictured as having roots as wide as the plant canopies, actually the roots spread wider, so mature plants benefit more from water applied at or just beyond the drip line than from water close to the trunk. (Anyway, watering too close to the trunk invites rot.)

When first establishing a large plant, however, be sure to get water directly to the root zone, which will be very close to the trunk. If the water is applied farther out, the roots may die before they spread to that point.

WATERING METHODS

The best techniques are those that keep the root crown and trunk dry—flooding a soil basin, inserting a deep-root irrigator, and using a drip system or soaker hoses. These methods are preferable to portable or underground sprinklers, which make it difficult to thoroughly water the root system without spraying the trunk.

BASINS. This is a good, no-runoff way to water a plant growing in open soil, with no lawn or ground cover planted around it. Form two concentric rings of soil and flood the outer ring as shown at left. On just-planted trees and shrubs, the outside ring should enclose the outer edge of the root ball; move it out as the plant grows.

DEEP-ROOT IRRIGATORS. Attached to a garden hose, a root irrigator injects water into the root zone, shooting it out horizontally in several directions below ground. It's an easy way to get supplemental water to a lawn tree—an efficiently irrigated lawn will only be moist to about 6 inches deep. Don't push the irrigator in deeper than 18 inches; position it about a third of the way in from the drip line, repeating this every few feet around the tree.

SOAKER HOSES. Arrange a soaker hose—either the flat perforated type, with the holes facing down, or the porous oozing type—in a spiral over the root zone for the most even coverage. The oozing type is best for level terrain and when hooked to a filter (to keep the pores from clogging) and a pressure regulator, though you can turn the faucet on low or place a washer in the soaker hose at the point of connection to reduce pressure.

Attached to a garden hose, the probelike deep-root irrigator injects water into the plant's root zone.

DRIP IRRIGATION. One of the easiest options is a ring of ½-inch emitter line placed at the tree's drip line. Rather than moistening just a few areas of the root zone, as widely spaced individual emitters will do, the emitter line will water all the way around the tree. Be sure to enlarge the ring as the tree grows. Minisprays are another good option. For specifics on setting up a drip system, see pages 68–84.

IRRIGATE UNDER EAVES

Don't rely on rain getting to foundation shrubs planted under house eaves—especially eaves that form deep overhangs. Check the moisture level at the root zone and water whenever necessary.

ROSES

It's often said that roses need the equivalent of 1 inch of rainfall each week for good growth and bloom, but actually they require moisture to the full depth of their roots (allow 16 to 18 inches)—which may amount to more than 1 inch. In rainy climates, don't assume that rainfall is always doing the job; check with a soil probe. When irrigating, apply water to root depth, again using a probe to see if you're succeeding. Ensure good drainage, because a waterlogged rose won't perform well.

Even in the dormant period, when plants are seemingly inactive, don't overlook watering. As long as the soil is not frozen, continue to water your roses as needed.

WATERING METHODS

Choose from the methods described below. In dry-summer climates, many gardeners who normally don't use overhead sprays on roses will occasionally sprinkle the leaves to cleanse them. In summer-rainfall areas, gardeners usually rely on rain to wash the foliage.

BASINS. Forming a soil basin that can hold around 2 or 3 gallons of water is a good way to water individual plants, though time-consuming if you have many roses. On level terrain, you can link the basins—turn the hose on low and let it fill the joined basins while you do something else.

PORTABLE SPRINKLERS. A common choice in summer-rainfall climates, a portable sprinkler may be wetting more than just your roses, especially if the plants are scattered throughout the garden. If they're situated among shallower-rooted plants, you may not be moistening them to root depth (check with a soil probe)—you may have to apply supplemental water or else water the other plants longer. To lessen the chance of foliar disease, sprinkle early in the day so that the leaves dry by nightfall.

UNDERGROUND SPRINKLER SYSTEMS. The sprinklers that water roses are usually part of a larger system covering lawns, flower beds, and other shrubs. Typically, stationary heads are chosen for roses and put on a separate irrigation circuit that waters plants with similar moisture needs. Run these sprinklers early in the day to discourage the development of leaf diseases. Flat-spray heads allow you to water without spraying the leaves. See pages 55–67 for more on sprinkler systems.

Operating at low pressure, these soaker hoses slowly ooze water over the root zones of rosebushes.

SOAKER HOSES. If your roses are situated on fairly level terrain, soaker hoses offer a simple way to water. When using the flat perforated type, place it hole side down (it spurts water with the holes up). The porous type will ooze water at low pressure; either hook it to a pressure regulator (and a filter to keep the pores from clogging), use a washer in the connection, or turn the water on low.

DRIP IRRIGATION. Both emitter line and individual emitters will apply water over the root zone and keep the leaves dry. To water a bed of closely spaced bushes, lay ½-inch emitter line in parallel rows: it will soak the whole bed.

For more widely spaced bushes, snake solid drip tubing to the plants you wish to irrigate; either encircle individual plants with ¼-inch emitter line that you connect to the drip tubing, or insert individual emitters directly into the tubing. You can choose adjustable emitters called bubblers that allow you to dispense water in streams rather than drips.

Microsprays are a third option—they spray water, but in smaller volumes and for shorter distances than conventional sprinklers. For more on drip systems, see pages 68–84.

Native Plants

The many types of native plants include those that grow wild in forests, woodlands, prairies, or deserts, or on the seashore or mountainsides of certain defined geographic regions. These plants survive on natural precipitation—and they will do so in your garden if given the same conditions they are used to in the wild.

The closer you stick to your locality when choosing native plants, the better your chances of success. If you live in Virginia and are considering some plants billed as southern natives, find out if they're actually indigenous to your part of the South. If you live in a state with diverse climates, such as California or Texas, be sure to choose plants accustomed to the climate and growing conditions of your specific region.

Soil is an especially important factor when growing natives. If the plant is used to dry, gravelly soil in the wild, that's what you should provide. If it's native to boggy soil, give it earth that will remain constantly moist.

In almost all cases, you'll have to irrigate native plants to get them established in your garden. In nature, these plants grow from seeds or from a parent plant's spreading roots or branches. But you're taking a nursery-raised plant with a small root system and plunking it into your garden, so it will need your help to become established. Once its roots are knitted into the soil (this may take one or two growing seasons), you can let nature take over. If your growing conditions don't quite mimic the wild conditions, you may have to do a little supplemental watering on a continuing basis.

Plants from various dry climates of the world thrive in this southwestern garden.

Native to the eastern central United States, purple coneflower *(Echinacea purpurea)* needs only moderate amounts of water.

WATERING METHODS

For native plants able to live on rainfall after they're established, one of the following temporary irrigation systems will suffice.

DRIP IRRIGATION. Because drip emitters keep the aboveground parts of plants dry, they are the best bet for watering natives sensitive to moisture around their root crowns. They are especially recommended for those accustomed to dry weather at the time you're irrigating them. You can use this system to water plants on any terrain, from level to very steep.

If you have a separate line going to the native plants, you can remove it entirely once the plants are established. To avoid needing an independent valve, put your natives on a branch of another line with a manual shutoff on the natives' branch. By turning off that part of the line whenever you want, you'll be able to control how much water the natives receive. At some point, you can simply eliminate that branch. See pages 68–84 for more on drip systems.

SOAKER HOSES. Soakers are an even simpler, less expensive method than a true drip system, though they won't water evenly on slopes. When irrigating plants that would ordinarily remain dry at that time of year, be sure to use a hose type that drips rather than sprays. If it's the kind with perforated holes, lay it hole side down. An ooze-type soaker should be operated at low pressure—use a pressure regulator (and a filter to keep the pores from clogging), insert a washer in the connection, or turn the water on low.

PORTABLE SPRINKLERS. Use this method only on natives that tolerate getting wet during the entire establishment period.

SEEDS AND STARTS

Without adequate water, seeds and young plants may die before their roots ever get established. A seed must soak up water in order to sprout, yet too much water will preclude the air it also needs to germinate. Once the seed grows into a young plant, it will require less water than a mature plant but, because of its small root system, will need it more frequently. When you transplant a seedling or other start into the garden, you must take care that it doesn't dry out between waterings. Also, apply that water gently so that it doesn't damage or knock over tender plants. Here's some advice for watering at various stages.

STARTING SEEDS INDOORS

Plant seeds (to the recommended depth for that plant type) in a porous, loose potting mix. After seeding the flats or other containers, set them in 1 or 2 inches of water and let them absorb water upward until the soil surface is moist; then drain the containers.

Uncovered containers will have to be misted regularly with a pump spray bottle to maintain humidity. Here's an easy way to create a moist greenhouse environment: place each container in a plastic bag or cover it with a sheet of glass. For ventilation, open the bags or remove the glass for 15 minutes daily. (You won't have to open the bags if you poke small holes in the tops.) As soon as the seeds have sprouted, remove the covering. Keep the soil moist but not soggy by misting or applying a very gentle spray.

Create a miniature greenhouse for trays of seeds by setting them in clear plastic bags until the seeds have sprouted. The bagged tray shown here is ready to emerge from its plastic cocoon. Once it's out, keep the potting mix moist but not soggy. When the seedlings have two sets of leaves, move them into their own pots; when the roots are established, the plants are ready to go into the garden. Maintain soil moisture throughout the process.

STARTING SEEDS IN THE GROUND

Plant the seeds in loose, crumbly soil that has been raked fine. To keep the seeds from washing away, water the seedbed with a fine-mist hose nozzle or with soaker hoses laid out in parallel rows to wet the entire bed. Tiny seeds barely covered with soil can be blanketed with a floating row cover or clear plastic sheeting to keep moisture in. Ventilate the plastic sheeting, and remove it as soon as the seeds sprout. Leave floating row covers in place if you want to protect the seedlings from cold or insects; you can water right through the material.

A "rose" on the watering can spout breaks the force of water applied to a celery seedling.

TRANSPLANTING

Water your seedlings or small nursery plants thoroughly before setting them in the garden. Before taking them out of their containers, prepare the holes: dig, fill with water, and let drain. After planting keep the soil moist, using the watering method recommended for that type of planting, until the plants are well rooted.

Sun and wind can dry out young plants quickly, so you may want to protect them with floating row covers or some other device. Water the established plants as required for that plant type.

CONTAINER PLANTS

Watering is the single most important job in container care. Potted plants have a limited amount of soil from which to draw moisture, and their roots are restricted by the pot size, so they require more frequent irrigation than do the same plants in the ground. Hanging pots require even more frequent watering than do pots on the ground, because air circulating around them dries out the soil faster.

One way to ensure even watering of a strawberry jar or other very deep container is to insert a "watering pipe." Use a piece of ¾ -inch PVC pipe about 4 inches longer than the height of your pot; drill small holes about every 2 inches along its length, and cap the bottom. Stand the pipe roughly in the center of the pot (without blocking the drainage hole) and plant the pot. To water the planted jar, pour water onto the soil surface and then into the pipe opening.

An easy way to decide whether a container plant needs water is to poke your finger into the top inch of soil; if it feels dry, it's time to water. With small pots, lifting the container is informative—the pot will feel lighter as the soil dries out. Plants will need extra watering in hot, dry, or windy weather. In blistering heat, some plants may need it more than once a day.

Moisten all the soil, not just the top few inches. You'll know the soil is saturated when water runs freely from the drainage hole. If water drains too fast, though, it's probably running down air space between dried-out soil and the container walls. To solve this problem, submerge the container in a tub of water for about half an hour. For a large pot, set a garden hose on the soil surface near the plant's base, adjust the flow to a trickle, and water for up to half an hour, until the soil is saturated.

Empty any saucer water within a few hours—water allowed to stand much longer will keep the soil soggy. Use a bulb-type baster to remove water from saucers under heavy containers.

WATERING METHODS

Use a method that delivers water directly to the soil and doesn't just hit the foliage or the outside of the pot, as conventional sprinklers might. Here are the best ways to water potted plants.

HAND WATERING. A watering can may be your choice if you have just a few containers. To keep water from splashing the soil, use a can with a "rose," a wide, perforated nozzle that sprinkles water gently. A watering can is also a convenient way to deliver water-soluble fertilizer.

Watering with a garden hose is faster than watering from a can, though it's still time-consuming if you have a lot of plants. Attach a nozzle that allows you to turn off the water between containers and also break up the force of the stream. A long-handled watering wand is helpful for long reaches.

For your deck or patio plants, you may want to try one of the new, space-saving, small-diameter hoses that attach to the kitchen

Use a watering wand to extend your reach.

faucet or a hose bibb. Some types are spiraled to stretch with you as you water. Be aware, however, that water flows from these hoses at a lower volume than from a standard garden hose, so watering will take longer.

SUBMERSION. Use this method on plants whose soil dries out quickly, such as those in small or hanging containers. A good soak will keep soil moist longer and revive plants whose soil has become dangerously dry. Lower the entire pot, up to its rim, into a tub of water and keep it there for about half an hour.

Dunk a hanging plant into a bucket of water to saturate the soil.

DRIP IRRIGATION. An automated drip line on its own valve makes it a cinch to water your potted plants frequently (as often as several times a day) and for short periods (usually from 2 to 5 minutes)—the watering regime under which they are most likely to thrive. You'll have to experiment to get the number and gallonage of emitters just right, so that water runs out of all the pots at about the same time.

A polyethylene supply line to your containers can run unobtrusively along a fence or wall or even under a deck (^{3}/$_8$-inch lines will be less noticeable than ^{1}/$_2$-inch lines). From the supply line, run microtubing to each container, threading it through the

These adjustable bubblers should be repositioned to water only the potting soil, or else their stream should be shortened by turning the cap.

drainage hole or up over the side of the pot. Depending on the size and shape of the container and the needs of its plants, the microtubing can connect to one or more drip emitters, ^{1}/$_4$-inch emitter line (or a homemade chain of mini in-line emitters), a small adjustable bubbler (an emitter that goes from droplets to a gentle stream), or a head that either sprays or mists. You can even install an system overhead to send tubes down into hanging pots.

For the microtubing, you can choose heavyweight vinyl instead of the standard polyethylene—the advantage of vinyl is that it will hug the contours of the container and turn corners without elbows or other fittings. Also, vinyl tubing comes in several colors to blend with the container color, whereas polyethylene tubing is typically black.

See pages 68–84 for specifics on setting up a drip system.

POT WISDOM

Here's how to keep potted plants from drying out too fast.

USE LARGE CONTAINERS. The larger the volume of soil, the slower it dries. (However, the watering interval will shorten once plant roots fill the soil.)

CHOOSE LESS POROUS MATERIALS. Water evaporates through unglazed clay, wood, and other porous pots. The least permeable pots are made of glazed pottery or plastic. You can seal a porous pot by painting the inside with asphalt roofing sealer or cement sealer.

ADD SOIL POLYMERS. They'll help the soil hold onto moisture longer; see page 15. In loose potting soil, they'll also facilitate the sideways spread of water from drip emitters.

MULCH THE SURFACE. To prevent the soil surface from drying out and repelling water, cover it with a layer of bark, compost, or pebbles.

DON'T GIVE A PLANT MORE SUN THAN IT NEEDS. If it thrives in either part shade or sun, give it part shade; it won't dry out as quickly.

Two pots, with mulch packed between, keep this tomato plant's roots cool.

DOUBLE UP POTS. Put the planted pot inside a larger empty one and fill the space between them with an insulating material such as gravel.

CLUSTER POTS. They'll shade and cool one another.

REPOT ROOTBOUND PLANTS. They dry out quickly. Trim the roots and replant into containers that are one size larger.

GLOSSARY

This manifold contains two antisiphon remote-control valves.

ANTISIPHON VALVE. A type of backflow preventer that creates an air gap. It is often incorporated into the control valve of an automated irrigation system.

ARC. The segment of a circle that a conventional sprinkler or microspray covers. For example, a head with a 180° arc sprays water in a half circle.

BACKFLOW PREVENTER. A device designed to keep water in irrigation pipes from flowing backward into the potable water system.

CIRCUIT. A section of an irrigation system served by its own separate control valve. Sometimes called a zone.

CONTROL VALVE. The device that regulates the flow of water from the irrigation main line to a particular circuit in an automated system.

DRAIN VALVE. A valve for emptying water from irrigation pipes, usually in preparation for winter.

ELBOW. An L-shaped fitting for making turns in pipe runs.

EMITTER LINE. Drip tubing containing factory-installed emitters spaced at regular intervals for soaking the ground.

EVAPOTRANSPIRATION (ET). Loss of water from the soil due to a combination of evaporation and transpiration (passage of water vapor through plant leaves).

FLOW RATE. The amount of water moving through pipes, measured in gpm or gph.

GPH. Gallons per hour; the output rate for drip emitters and microsprays.

GPM. Gallons per minute; the output rate for conventional sprinklers.

HOSE BIBB. An outdoor faucet.

HYDROZONE. An area containing groups of plants sharing the same moisture needs.

IRRIGATION MAIN LINE. Pipe running from the service line to a system's control valves; it always contains water and thus is under constant pressure.

LATERAL LINE. Pipe or tubing running from each control valve to the sprinklers or drip-watering devices on that circuit; it contains water only when that circuit is in operation.

MANIFOLD. A cluster of control valves for multiple circuits.

MICROTUBING. Narrow-diameter (¼- and ⅛-inch) drip tubing.

NIPPLE. A short length of threaded pipe used for sprinkler risers and for joining closely spaced threaded irrigation components.

POINT OF CONNECTION. The place where you connect your irrigation system to your house water supply.

POLYETHYLENE. A flexible plastic pipe or tubing.

PRECIPITATION RATE. The number of inches per hour at which water is applied.

PRESSURE REGULATOR. A device for reducing the water pressure within an irrigation system or within individual circuits.

PSI. Pounds per square inch: the measurement of water pressure.

PVC. Polyvinyl chloride, a type of rigid plastic used for irrigation pipe and fittings.

REMOTE-CONTROL VALVE. A control valve wired to a timer that can be programmed to open and close that valve automatically.

RISER. A short length of threaded pipe or other upright support for a conventional sprinkler or microspray, connecting it to the lateral line.

ROTORS. Rotary sprinkler heads of gear-driven or impact design used for watering large areas.

SERVICE LINE. The water pipe running from the supplier's main line to your house.

STATION. A terminal on a timer, or controller, that can be programmed to operate the control valve to which it is wired. You can have as many control valves (and circuits) as there are stations on your timer.

TEE. A T-shaped fitting with three openings, for branching pipe lines and for connecting sprinkler risers to underground pipe.

THROW RADIUS. The distance that a sprinkler or microspray disperses water, measured from the head to the outer part of the arc.

WATER PRESSURE. The force of water in a piping system, measured in pounds per square inch (psi). Static pressure is the force when water is at a standstill; dynamic, or working, pressure is the force when water is flowing.

RESOURCE GUIDE

The entities listed here are among the many sources of watering products and information. Also check local nurseries, garden centers, and home-improvement and hardware stores for watering tools and irrigation-system components.

STORES AND CATALOGS

Each of the following sells by mail order and in at least one retail outlet.

THE GARDENER'S SUPPLY COMPANY
128 Intervale Road
Burlington, VT 05401
800-955-3370
www.gardeners.com
Watering tools, rain barrels

HARMONY FARM SUPPLY
3244 Gravenstein Highway
Sebastopol, CA 95472
707-823-9125
www.harmonyfarm.com
Sprinkler and drip-irrigation supplies

LEE VALLEY TOOLS, LTD.
800-871-8158 (U.S.)
800-267-8767 (Canada)
www.leevalley.com
Watering tools, soaker hoses, rain barrels; stores located in Canada

A. M. LEONARD, INC.
241 Fox Drive
Piqua, OH 45356
800-543-8955
www.amleo.com
Watering tools, soil probes, soil moisture meters

THE NATURAL GARDENING COMPANY
217 San Anselmo Avenue
San Anselmo, CA 94960
707-766-9303
www.naturalgardening.com
Watering tools, soaker hoses, drip-irrigation kits

SMITH & HAWKEN
800-776-3336
www.smith-hawken.com
Watering tools

THE URBAN FARMER STORE
2833 Vicente Street
San Francisco, CA 94116
415-661-2204; 800-753-3747
653 East Blithedale Avenue
Mill Valley, CA 94941
415-380-3840
Sprinkler and drip-irrigation supplies

MANUFACTURERS

The following can direct you to local distributors of their products; many will also provide catalogs or other publications.

AGRIFIM IRRIGATION PRODUCTS, INC.
337 West Bedford Avenue
Fresno, CA 93711
209-431-2003
www.agrifimusa.com
"Smart Watering" booklet on drip irrigation (for sale)

AQUAPORE MOISTURE SYSTEMS INC., A FISKARS COMPANY
610 South 80th Avenue
Phoenix, AZ 85043
800-635-8379
www.aquapore.com
Soaker hoses, sprinkler hoses, drip-irrigation products

DRIWATER
50 Old Courthouse Square
Suite 606
Santa Rosa, CA 95404
707-528-WATER
www.driwater.com
Gelled, slow-release water

HUNTER INDUSTRIES
1940 Diamond Street
San Marcos, CA 92069
760-744-5240
www.hunterindustries.com
Sprinkler-irrigation products; design and installation guide

LAWNBELT IRRIGATION PRODUCTS
1422 Irwin Drive
Erie, PA 16505
888-283-8850
No-trenching, freezeproof sprinkler system in a kit

NETAFIM USA
5470 East Home Avenue
Fresno, CA 93727
800-777-6541
www.netafim-usa.com
Drip-irrigation products

NIBCO IRRIGATION SYSTEMS
2851 East Florence Avenue
Fresno, CA 93721
209-485-7171
www.nibcoirrigation.com/turfbubbler
Wick-irrigation system for lawns

OLSON IRRIGATION SYSTEMS
10910 Wheatlands Avenue
Santee, CA 92071
800-77OLSON
Drip-irrigation products

ORBIT IRRIGATION PRODUCTS, INC.
P. O. Box 328
Bountiful, UT 84011
800-488-6156
www.orbit-irrigation.com
Hose-end, sprinkler, and drip-irrigation products

RAIN BIRD
Technical Services
800-247-3782
www.rainbird.com
Landscape irrigation products

RAINDRIP
2250 Agate Court
Simi Valley, CA 93065
800-367-3747 (California)
800-222-3747 (other states)
www.raindrip.com
"Drip Watering Made Easy" booklet

REWATER SYSTEMS, INC.
477 Marina Parkway
Chula Vista, CA 91910
619-585-1196
Gray-water underground drip-irrigation systems

THE TORO COMPANY
Irrigation Division
5825 Jasmine Street
Riverside, CA 92504
800-644-4740
www.toro.com
Landscape irrigation products

WATER RIGHT
972 Coronado Drive
Costa Mesa, CA 92626
949-724-1048
Soil probes

ADDITIONAL WEBSITES

www.atinet.org/cati/cit
Articles about irrigation

www.irri-gate.com
Search engine for irrigation questions

www.irrigation.org
General irrigation information

www.wateright.org
ET-based watering schedules for California (with other western states to be added)

INDEX